The Legacy of Karl Marx

Murzban Jal

AAKAR

The Legacy of Karl Marx
Murzban Jal

First Published 2020

ISBN 978-93-5002-654-0

Published by
AAKAR BOOKS
28 E Pocket IV, Mayur Vihar Phase I
Delhi 110 091 India
aakarbooks@gmail.com

Laser Typeset at
Sakshi Computers, Delhi

Printed at
D.K. Fine Art Press, Delhi 110052

Acknowledgements

I would like to thank the Indian Institute of Education, Pune and the Indian Council of Social Science Research, New Delhi, both legendary institutes dealing with social science research in the continuous support to scientific research that has lead to the writing of this book. Also thanks to N. Anjaiah on whose inspiration this book emerged.

The Legacy of Karl Marx

> On close consideration, Marxism is not just another hypothesis that might be replaced tomorrow by some other. It is the philosophy of history and to renounce it is to dig the grave of Reason in history.
>
> Maurice Merleau-Ponty, *Humanism and Terror.*

> The left is undergoing a shattering experience: the progressive movement is being compelled to invent its whole project. What tends to be forgotten, however, is that a similar experience gave birth to Leninism.
>
> Slavoj Žižek, 'Seize the Day: Lenin's: Legacy'.

Rethinking Historical Materialism as a "Revolution with a Revolution"

Revolution with a Revolution, delightful revolution, authentic revolution, unique revolution where the real explosion of freedom as the expression of the beautiful moment of universal solidarity burst forth. Revolution without a Revolution, tragic revolution, or simply no revolution, sadness, melancholia, mourning...... What does re-thinking historical materialism as a Revolution with a Revolution mean? It means following the legacy or should one say legacies of Marx, not spectre or spectres of Marx, because though there is the spectre of communism haunting the world, there is no spectre of Marx. One follows the spectre of communism in Cairo, Tehran, Gadchiroli, the World Bank and the global stock exchanges....follows them where we understand our present times. Let us thus move to present times.

The present times could be best suited to understand the legacy of Marx. On the one hand, the form of evangelic messianic capitalism that Francis Fukuyama celebrated as the reign of the "last man", as he so infamously expressed it, where the "end of history" had somehow miraculously come, has been realized in the global economic crisis. This form of messianic capitalism is ironically the story of the destruction of not only messianic capitalism promoted by neo-liberalism, but the destruction of capitalism as such. For what messianic capitalism in announcing the end of history and the complete death of Marxism did was in an ironical way 'return' to the early part of the 20th century, in search for its neo-liberal roots.

In this miraculous return, capitalism not only saw the figures of the liberals and the conservatives, the popes and the czars marching in this scene of history, but also the figures of Lenin, Rosa Luxemburg, Trotsky and other figures that comprise the entire repertoire of Revolutionary Marxism. The revolution that was chased and exorcised by the global counterrevolutionaries has returned once more. The theme of the promised fall of global capitalism and the victory of the proletariat that Marx and Engels announced in the *Communist Manifesto*[1] has also returned to delight us once again.

If the delight in spotting the return of the revolution comprises the first site of Marx's legacy, we also have a second site. In this site we do not see the figure of what one may call the "revolutionary delight", but the figure of "reactionary melancholia". This figure is the figure of the counterrevolution and the counterrevolutionary. It stares at us, it haunts us.

This counterrevolutionary figure moans that there can be no immediate abolishing of commodity production, no smashing of the state. It claims that the dictatorship of the proletariat can only be the dictatorship of the party over the proletariat. It claims that Marxism can only be totalitarianism of the worst sort. It suggests that one joins the parliament. It claims that Lenin was good, but does not talk of Lenin's idea of "parliamentary cretinism". It says that Marx was right when he talked of the proletariat as the international multitude, but his internationalism was said to exist in some bygone era. Now, so the figure of reactionary melancholia claims, is the era of socialism in one country, even socialism is one state, socialism introduced by the parliament.

We have now the culmination of this reactionary melancholia: the collapse of the Soviet Union and the figure of Fukuyama along with the children of Samuel Huntington celebrating the miraculous end of history. It is here that we talk of the legacy of Marx. To talk of the legacy of Marx is to talk of the truth of Marx: of the general law of capital accumulation, of the concentration of capital that leads to monopoly capitalism and the formation of global cartels culminating in imperialism. But there are also other truths, truths quite often forgotten: of the permanent revolution, the impossibility of socialism in one country, the great difficulties for a revolution in a backward country to succeed independent of a revolution in Europe, etc. It is with these truths that one turns to another legacy of Marx, what Slavoj Žižek calls the "politics of truth".[2] This politics of truth is real. It is not a "politics of memory"[3]. We are unlike Derrida trying to remember Marx, trying to pay a debt to this great thinker. We are in no state of mourning.

Our thesis will be dialectical, to be precise grounded in dialectical materialism. It will not be sectarian. Instead it will recall the great Hegelian dictum: "truth lies in the whole". We will in no way be sectarian, i.e. not only political sectarian that has unfortunately plagued the left movement after Lenin's death, but also philosophically sectarian. Instead we shall be Marxist, even take a form of a "Marxology" where we try to read Marx as far as possible in the original German, try to fathom what his theory of alienation implies in the pathology of everyday life, what the relation is between alienation and the problem of the fetishism of commodities and both these with class struggle and the acquiring of class consciousness. We also try to read not only the relation between his earlier works and *Capital*, but also bring in his understanding of non-Western societies, especially a reading of his rather unknown work *The Ethnological Notebooks.* In this sense the question of caste, the Indian village communities and the relation between caste and modern classes comes in prominently.

This would be a brief form of Marxology. But besides this form of a scholarly understanding of Marx, one also reads and thinks of the brilliance of Engels, Lenin, Luxemburg, Trotsky, Bukharin, Gramsci, not to forget what would soon to be called "Western Marxism" from the Frankfurt School, via Louis Althusser to Žižek. This space of Marxology is vast and no matter how much wants to fill in, the space is just too vast to be covered in a few sentences. There is however a type of a restricted tragedy which I think Perry Anderson brought out in his *In the Tracts of Historical Materialism.* Here he said that "Western Marxism" in being born from the reaction to Stalinism, went from the site of the critique of political economy to almost some form of culture theory in the academic and non-revolutionary (if not anti-revolutionary) sense.

It was Isaac Deutscher who had said somewhere that in terms of sheer brilliance, one could not compare Lenin, Rosa Luxemburg, Leon Trotsky and Bukharin with thinkers who followed them. In a certain sense one could claim this to be an exaggeration. In another sense there could be nothing but realism in this observation. Marx produced Marxism, Lenin produced Leninism, Trotsky created Trotskyism, etc. Could one say that Max Weber produced Weberism, Dilthey Dilteheyism, or Habermas produced Habermasism? Why is that we need to think this very radical difference?

One thus begins with what is called "academic politics"[4]. We, and I mean, the 'we' in this hall of philosophical Marxism, want to deal with Marx, with Marxism and the entire legacy of Marxism. We do not deal with academic politics, but with Revolutionary Marxism. Yet we turn back to this academic politics, as well as we desire to turn away not only from this academic politics, but academics in general. We wish to turn to what Jacques Lacan calls the "Real", to be precise to the *Real of the Revolution*. We then want a *Revolution with a Revolution*. One knows that it was Robespierre who chided the democrats of the French Revolution who wanted a *Revolution without a Revolution.* The question that we pose is: how does one reinvent this radical idea of the *Revolution with a Revolution*? And will we be morally accountable for this great act?

It is from the posing of this question that one tries to conceptualize what the radical legacy of Marx means. One only has to look at the crises of capitalism and the struggles in Greece, Spain and Portugal, not to forget from South America to Iran and Egypt, to understand what Marx meant by the general law of capital accumulation and the crisis emerging thereof. One also has to see the heroic struggles against a theological-fascist regime in Iran by the left secular forces and think how right Lenin was in *What is to be Done?* that a party of professional revolutionaries trained in the finest and most modern theory could realize a Revolution with a Revolution.

At the outset let it be noted that Marxism is to be understood as historicism and humanism that rejects all forms of mechanical materialism, not to forget the entire metaphysics of Stalinism and the Soviet school of manipulating Marxism, as well as all forms of revolutionary terrorism. One needs to understand that Marx emphasized communism as a fully developed humanism and naturalism and that Marxism was nothing but the appropriating of the human essence, and that Marx's communism as a fully developed humanism and naturalism is nothing but Lenin's insurrection as art.[5] In this sense one is trying to comprehend a Marxist aesthetical politics.

I am reiterating these points not only to articulate the deep relation between Marx's *Economic and Philosophic Manuscripts of 1844* (remember that this was published only in 1932 and that Lenin never knew of this text) and Lenin's party of professional revolutionaries. It is in this space that one re-thinks Marx's legacy and articulates how to re-think historical materialism as seeking a Revolution with a Revolution.

To conceptualize the legacy of Marx, to comprehend the science of Marx, and thus the scientific truth that capitalism is crisis-ridden, is also to understand how this science can be transformed into an aesthetical politics. We are taking this theme from Lenin's *Marxism and Insurrection* where the art of insurrection was put up. In this sense we will not only understand the crisis-related theme, but understand it in the stage of tragicomic history. For Marx the crisis is not a mere crisis, but an *absurd crisis*.[6] This absurd crisis is struck by a type of disease, an epidemic, the "epidemic of overproduction".[7] This epidemic is constituted by a type of surplus produced, a surplus that one calls "defecation"[8], where the observation "there is too much civilization, too much subsistence, too much industry, too much commerce"[9] is transformed simply as "there is too much defecation". We are struck by the ailment of "momentary barbarism".[10] Earlier we were barbarians waiting to be civilized. *Now we are civilized barbarians!* And because we are saying that

Marx's science is being experimented on the stage of tragicomic history and because we claim that there is a very close relation between not only art and politics (in the aesthetics of insurrection) but also claim that there is a dramaturgy in Marx's science, we will transform Hegel's dictum "truth lies in the whole" into the dialectical holism of science, arts and ethics. Marxism as dialectical and historical materialism becomes a dramaturgy where the drama of the spectre of communism coming to haunt not only Europe but the entire world is being played out.

It is in this sense that we will let a very radical form of Marxism intervene–Marxism-Leninism to be precise, where the party of insurrection will realize communism as humanism and naturalism. And because, as we noted earlier, that with messianic capitalism announcing the return of liberalism, the irony of this repeating history postulated a counter perspective to the liberal narrative: not the return of the bankers, popes and czars, but the return of the revolutionaries, thus the return of Leninism and the revolutionary party. And because with the return of Lenin one sees as complete bourgeois intolerance against both radical politics and Leninism, one has another form of intolerance: Leninist intolerance, intolerance to global capitalism, and to liberals, neo-cons and fascists alike. Here I recall Žižek's notion of Leninist intolerance.[11] Tolerance' is not about real tolerance, not about real humanity, not about equality of all religions, etc. which the state always preaches and never practises. 'Tolerance' here is about the spectacle of capitalism, about forgetting revolution, forgetting the overproduction of commodities and with it the overproduction of the regression of critical thinking. Leninist intolerance is about this very radical critique of regressive thinking. So when Lenin had said in *What is to be Done?* that one has to seek a modern science, a Theory (with a capital "T"), he also meant that one had to always combat this regressive thinking. Lenin calls it "the most advanced theory".[12]

One does not only have to combat the ideologies of the czars and the popes, not only combat royalty and religion. One has to combat this tolerance for the popes and the czars, of royalty and religion. To be humanist, in the very Marxist sense, one has to be combative, combative of this liberal notion of tolerance. It ponders over the following three observations:

> Democracy is a contradiction in itself, an untruth, nothing but hypocrisy at the bottom. Political liberty is sham liberty, the worst form of slavery...The contradiction must come out....(in the form of) real equality....(in the form of) communism[13].
>
> If democracy, in essence, means the abolition of class domination, then why should not a socialist minister charm the whole bourgeois world by oration on class collaborations? Why should he not remain in the cabinet even after the shooting-down of workers by gendarmes has exposed for the hundredth and thousand times, the real nature of the democratic collaboration of classes?[14]

and,

> Fidelity to the democratic consensus means the acceptance of the present liberal-parliamentary consensus, which precludes any serious questioning of how this liberal-democratic order is complicit in the phenomena it officially condemns and, of course, any serious attempt to imagine a society whose socio-political order would be different.[15]

It is this very juncture that I articulate historical materialism as a Revolution with a Revolution from a very different perspective than what usually Marxists, post-Lenin, thought. We talk of a New Science of desireology that perfects the art of insurrection that transcends the Old Science of ideology. We claim that the Old Discipline is thought, and only thought. The ideologists thought that the whole world is comprised of thoughts and to change the world, one only had to change thoughts. What did the ideologists do? They thought of revolution, a revolution that occurred many times each day in their terribly clever craniums.

Their revolution–i.e. the revolution of the ideologists–was a Revolution without a Revolution. We know that Marx and Engels wrote an entire tome of it called *The German Ideology*. We also know that Engels called ideology "false consciousness"[16]. And yet we somehow claim that Marxism is an ideology.

Turning from "Ideology" to "Desireology"

We turn away from academic politics and thus turn away from the ideologies and the whole world of pure fantasies to the Real of the Revolution. In this sense we become materialists by turning away from the "Imaginary" and the "Symbolic" to the "Real". In this turning to the realm of the Real, we become desireologists. We must confess that this may seem to be an almost embarrassing term. I had used this in an article in the *Economic and Political Weekly* where I said that ideology as both a discipline and a practice is always predicted on the commodity and that ideology is both a false consciousness, as also what we know since psychoanalysis as the "repressed unconscious"[17]. Consider this classical definition:

> Ideology is a process accomplished by the so-called thinker consciously, it is true, but with a false consciousness. The real motive forces impelling him remain unknown to him: otherwise would not be an ideological process. Here he imagines false or seeming motive forces. Because it is a process of thought he derives its form as well as content from pure thought, either his own or his predecessors. He works with mere thought material, which he accepts without examination as the product of thought, and he does not investigate further for a more remote source independent of thought; indeed it is a course to, because all action is *mediated* by thought, it appears to him to be ultimately based on thought[18].

To understand this question of ideology and the problematic of "mere thought"–we could provisionally call it: "surplus thought"–we turn to Lenin in Capri in 1908 three years after the defeated 1905 revolution. The revolution is defeated, repression is at its height and the ultra-left section of the Bolsheviks–Lunacharsky and company–begin to think that "matter has disappeared". They call themselves the "God-seekers". Though they are philosophically conservative, politically they are almost anarchist–they want to abstain from politics. Gorky is also influenced by this god-seeking, politically abstaining philosophy. He meets Lenin and asks him for a "philosophical offer". He wants Lenin to discuss with the 'disappearing anti-materialists'. Lenin's answer? He laughs. We call this Lenin's philosophical laughter. Lenin does not want to talk of philosophy. He thinks that philosophical discussions would weaken the Bolsheviks. But Lenin does write a small tome on philosophy where he defines philosophy as a *Holzweg* or a false path. Not only does Lenin want to claim that philosophy is a false path, it is the "falsest of false paths" (*Holzweg der Holzwege*) and the "professors of philosophy" are "graduated flunkeys" who "stultify people by their torturous 'idealism'"[19]. Philosophers are not only graduated flunkeys, but also torturers. They torture with their idealisms. They become like Shakespeare's Cassius:

> Yond Cassius has a lean and hungry look,
> *He thinks too much; such men are dangerous.*[20]

So what does Lenin propose to do? He of course does not want to think too much. Instead he proposes a different practice of philosophy. Now we know that Althusser has focused on both Lenin and the different practice of philosophy. But Althusser himself being an academic philosopher cannot conceive what this different practice is. He cannot understand dialectical materialism and Marx's tremendous scientific revolution because he himself remains an academic. He does not understand the relation between science and aesthetics. He can most certainly talk of the revolution, but he cannot talk of the Revolution with a Revolution. He thus cannot link philosophy–especially the different practice of philosophy–with class struggle. He remains an ideologist. He cannot understand what radical philosophy is, what the Leninist party is, what the most modern science is.

It is from this conjuncture that we turn to the construction of a radical philosophy that grasps the masses by the roots. In this sense we turn from philosophy as torturous idealism to radical praxis. For this we need to understand what the young Marx had once said. According to Marx, a radical break is necessary in human understanding. One has to have a complete upheaval. So to understand philosophy one has to learn the art of literally transcending philosophy by realizing it. Now what does this mean? It means that one learns praxis, to be precise, revolutionary praxis.

But then what is the relation between philosophy–to be precise Marxist philosophy, or the theory that Lenin talked of without which there could be no revolution–and revolutionary praxis? To understand this one needs to go into Marx's celebrated revolution in philosophy and the formation that he had outlined in his *Contribution to the Critique of Hegel's Philosophy of Right. Introduction*. Before we understand the two terms in German (in this text) that form the basics of revolutionary dialectics, it is important that one needs to understand what is called the "most radical rupture with traditional ideas"[21]. It is this grand paradigm shift, this "terrain shift" that Althusser loved calling, whereby one understands both the different practice of philosophy as well the possibilities of revolutionary praxis.

Let us look at these two terms: (1) *Aufhebung* that is translated as "sublation-transcendence-supersession", and (2) *Verwirklichung* which implies simply an "actualization" or "realization". The first one is what Hegel had introduced in his *Science of Logic* where he talked of *Aufhebung* as a process essential embedded in history (in fact which forms the basics of the motor force of history). Now according to this dialectical logic of *Aufhebung* reality is "lifted up" at a higher level of existence through the double process of cancellation and preservation. Both Marxist philosophy and revolutionary praxis "lifts up" reality at a higher level, the level from capitalism and the dehumanization of the production of commodities into the site of world revolution.

Now every Marxist should understand this dialectics of history in order to situate oneself in a proper historical context. What I have called the politics of revolutionary desire–or simply desireology–is constituted in this dialectics of history. And that is why I have slightly modified the philosophy and science of dialectical and historical materialism as *dialectical and historical-humanist materialism.* In more than one way I relate this with Gramsci's historicism and humanism and Raya Dunayevskaya's Marxist-Humanism. In the most prominent way Marxism then is understood as the critique of mechanical materialism and the theory of the "iron laws" of history. One develops a philosophy of praxis. The Communist Party, to be precise, the Marxist-Leninist Party, becomes the party of action. It transforms the Enlightenment theme of the "'man' of action" into the theory of the *party of action*. Our theme will now flow to this site of the party of action which understands the role of the party as what Karl Korsch once called, "*human sensuous activity, as praxis*"[22].

It is here that one is able to differentiate the revolutionary Leninist party from the parties of revisionism and parliamentary democracy. In contrast to these revisionists who more than dealing with dynamic social reality, deal with the realm of the 'ideological' (and the fixation with 'ideas'), Revolutionary Marxism teaches us the materialization and humanization of 'ideas'. It does not talk of the 'ideas' of god, the soul, the nature of reality, etc. instead it talks of what the good society should be all about and say that communism is this good society. And because Marxism is always people-friendly and because it puts the hopes and desires of humanity at the centre of its revolutionary politics, it learns to encounter the collective conscious of the working masses as well as the deep unconscious. What we now say is that Marxism should not at all deal with 'consciousness' and 'ideologies'. Instead one goes into the deep desires of the working masses. One then goes to the triple critiques of human alienation (the split of one human from the other), political economy (the study of the accumulation of capital) and the unconscious (what our desires are all about).

To understand this let us deepen the Marxist understanding of ideology as false consciousness. We have this concept now being further realized as the new definition of ideology that emerges in *Capital*: "We are not aware of this, nevertheless we do it". (*Sie wissen das nicht, aber sie tun es*)[23]. Ideology is thus not about being aware, but it is about the repression of this awareness. If on the one hand we are dealing with the politics of the unconscious, we have now with the triumph of the global Media Industry a new definition of ideology: "They know it, yet they do it!"[24] Now the Marxist revolutionary will have to understand that it is both these contexts that have to be dealt with. We have to deal with the unconscious (the first definition from Marx: ideology is unawareness, the realm of the unconscious) as well as with a type of what we know after Žižek as an "enlightened false consciousness" or simply a petty bourgeois cynicism.

And that is also why we say, as we had earlier said, that one understands the unconscious and then moves from the politics of the unconscious to the revolutionary site of desire.[25] And that is also why we say that Revolutionary Marxism is all about revolutionary desire. When Lenin insisted in *What is to be Done?* on the role of the professional revolutionary he implied the art of desiring, that leads to the aesthetics of insurrection. This art is primarily a solution to bourgeois cynicism and to the spectacle of late imperialism in permanent crisis. One is not dealing any more with 'consciousness', the consciousness whether Narendra

Modi is good or not good. One is now in the midst of desire. Thus one is not interested any more in changing 'consciousness'. The left ideologist who intends to 'teach' the worker about his/her own situation is nothing but the bourgeois educator who remains perpetually bourgeois. In this sense we transcend not only the mechanical types of politics that were evident in Bukharin, but also transcend the problem of the reification of consciousness that Lukács made central to his *History and Class Consciousness.*

So what do we do? We claim that instead of ideas and ideologies (even Lukács' reified consciousness), one puts "the real, corporeal *human being*" with its "real objective *essential powers*" (*wirklichen gegenstandlichen Wesenkräfte*)[26] at the centre of revolutionary politics. Marx's will to revolutionary power that produces the moment of what one may call the "revolutionary sublime moment" now enters the scene of revolution. Now what we do is claim that instead of ideologies we have the *natural powers* (*naturlichen Kräften*) and *vital powers* (*Lebenskräften*)"[27], or simply "human essential powers" (*menschlichen Wesenkrafte*)[28] that firstly generates and then celebrates the revolutionary sublime moment. And it is this legacy that Lenin picks up. Marx's idea of human essential powers of the working class that comprehends a mass struggle against capitalism, is realized as the party of *direct action*. We use this term "desireology" so as to understand the relation between science and art–especially on the idea of human sensibility of Marx's *Economic and Philosophic Manuscripts of 1844.* If classical aesthetics deals with the beautiful and the culture industry deals with the ridiculous–what the Frankfurt School called "pacifying rebellious desire"–desireology as the art of insurrection deals with what Lenin in *April Thesis* called the *Augenblick* or the unique chance of revolution.[29]

And since the "ontological essence of human passion (*Leidenschaft*) coming into being"[30] is now our focus, we say that the revolutionary party is also the party of sublime passion. The world revolution is the realization of this passion. Passion is of course related to humanity at large, with humanity as humanity. It is this humanity as humanity which Marx called, "the human essence" (*das menschliche Wesen*) and communism as the realization of this human essence. Understanding this humanism of Marx one claims that the question of the good society is central to Marxism. Of course we know that this understanding has not to be confused with utopian conceptions, for any references to what one may vaguely call 'stupid sentiments' is alien to Marxism. I keep this idea of the good society that is devoid of 'stupid sentiments' as not only central, but also central in a very contradictory way. Recall what Lenin had said to Gorky about the great European composer Beethoven so as to understand this contradiction:

> "I know the *Appassionata* (this is a Beethoven piano sonata, my insertion, M.J.) inside out and yet I am willing to listen to it every day. It is wonderful, ethereal music. On hearing it I proudly, maybe somewhat naively, think: See! People are able to produce such marvels!" He then winked, laughed and added sadly: "I'm often unable to listen to music, it gets on my nerves, I would like to stroke my fellow beings and whisper sweet nothings in their ears for being able to produce such beautiful things in spite of the abominable hell they are living in. However, today one shouldn't caress anybody–for people will only bite off your hand; strike, without pity, although theoretically we are against any kind of violence. Umph, it is, in fact, an infernally difficult task!"[31]

And it is this "infernally difficult task" of wanting to caress people living in "abominable hell", and yet striking without pity (though theoretically being against violence) that propels us to see what Marx discovered, such that one "strikes without pity" even when you want to "stroke my fellow beings".

On Marx's Dramaturgy of Replaying Hamlet

We are caught in this moral dilemma. And it is in this moral dilemma that we recall Lenin as the critic of liberalism and parliamentary democracy. We also recall Shakespeare's Hamlet, Hamlet as the Prince of Liberalism and Parliamentary Democracy.

To bring in Lenin on the scene of revolution we owe of course to the fighting comrades. We also owe to not only Lukács, but also Žižek and Lars Lih. But remember Lenin is feared and loathed and Leninism feared even more.[32] So fearful is the state to Leninism that the Indian state has said in one of its awful fits of frights that they are terrorists and the "single biggest security threat to Indian security". Along with the illiberal popes and czars our very liberal Prime Minister hates communism. He hates those who are against corporate capitalism, against the SEZS, against the parliamentary system. He disagrees with Lenin's theory of "parliamentary cretinism". For him communists are ghosts of a bygone age. In a certain sense with this theme of fear and horror cropping up, the celebrated theme of the spectre of communism coming to haunt us emerges once again. The spectre of communism haunts. But it also taunts. It brings in fear to the world bourgeoisie. In this sense there is a drama constructed. Let us have a look at it.

In this dramaturgy, Marx poses a counter to this spooky tale. The spectre is not a real spectre, but a real force, comprised of real people. The story of communism being a ghost is a "nursery tale" made up by the popes and global czars. Instead Marx says that it is capitalism that is spooky, that it is unreal, or to be precise, anti-humanist. Remember in the very first pages of *Capital* he says that the very essence of capitalism is comprised of mere ghostly reality that is devoid of not only real humans, but is also a hyper-reality devoid of material reality. Or to be precise, he says that capitalism breaks the material world and creates an artificial, immaterial, hypostasized world. In this unreal, anti-humanist world governed by what Marx calls "magic and necromancy,"[33] we have people being trampled on and Monsieur Capital as the Master Ghost doing his ghost walk all over the world[34]. What happens in this dramaturgy is that humanity at large is struck by what the young Marx called the "estranged mind".

What we do now is relate the actual scene of Indian politics—mainly the parliamentary politics with the case of the people struck by the epidemic of the estranged mind and the Master Ghost walker Monsieur Capital who seizes land for corporate capitalism and declares all resistance as terrorist activity—with the dramaturgy that we are reconstructing. We shall contextualize this drama. If ancient popes and modern ministers think that the Red Spectre is going to destroy the holy world and private property (the holiest of the holy), then those who thought that they were Marxists, but confused by the terrible trio of Bernstein, Kautsky and Stalin, think that another holy place, the parliament as the modern temple, is the site of revolutionary practice. In this sense we see Hamlet appearing once again. If we said that we owe Lukács, Žižek and Lars Lih, we now owe to Derrida who related Marx with Shakespeare's Hamlet.

Hamlet is a Prince, as we know it. But he is also a bourgeois in the era of the transition of feudalism to capitalism. Re-contextualizing Hamlet in the age of late capitalism, he becomes the Prince of neo-liberal capitalism. Yet he rejects this crown. He believes in the philosophy of the welfare state. He likes Nehru, even the parliamentary leftists. But he is totally confused, as existentialist ethics is his paradigm of action. It is said in Shakespeare's original tragedy that a ghost is seen. It could be an apparition, even an illusion. The ghost/apparition/illusion is of his father killed in a fratricidal act.

We have thus three characters: the ghost (a sort of surplus that has not yet faded away): he is the true sovereign who is challenged by his own brother. This brother is a typical politician found in the Indian parliament in the age of globalization and communalism. He is the New Machiavelli who converts the welfare state into a police state, suppressing trade unions, engineering riots, and above all killing the real sovereign, the welfare state built on Constitutional Democracy. This New Machiavelli kills Nehruvian politics, the NAM, tries to kill the project of secularism. Hamlet is the third character. He is the child of the ghost, the child of the welfare state, who is haunted by the ghost of welfare capitalism. He cannot see ahead. He cannot see Marxism and the proletariat revolution. In fact every idea of revolution is alien to him.

Turn this Shakespearean Marxist text to contemporary times and ask the question: "Who is Hamlet?" The response is not the children of Nehru, but his distinct nephews: the Indian parliamentary leftists. Our Indian Hamlet, our parliamentary leftist is like the original Hamlet, simply unable to act and is traumatized by the illusions plaguing his mind. Like the original Hamlet he cannot revolt, since revolution is alien to him, since he fears that the New Sovereign will declare him to be a terrorist. He then wants to be part of the establishment that he hates. The secret of this drama can be found here where we are told to:

> ....have recourse to the mist enveloped regions of the religious world. In that world the products of the human brain appear as independent beings (*selbständige Gestalten*) endowed with life and entering into relations with one another and the human race. So it is in the world of commodities with the products of men's hands. That is what I call the Fetishism which attaches to the products of labour, so soon as they are produced as commodities, and which is therefore inseparable from the production of commodities[35].

Freud, Marx and the Question of Hamlet's Alienation

So we see that Hamlet is seized by "independent beings (*selbständige Gestalten*) endowed with life". He is terrorized by these very strange beings. He becomes, what Jean Hyppolite's once called, a "mentally estranged person", caught in the "enchanted topsy-turvy world" where "Monsieur le Capital and Madame la Terre do their ghost-walking".[36] He seeks to flee. He curses the very day he was born:

> The time is out of joint; O cursed spite,
> That ever I was born to set it right![37]

He is reified, not as an insect as in Kafka's *Metamorphosis*, but as some sort of modern 'man' who lives in "the world of illusions, half-truths and unsolved contradictions feeling completely at home in these estranged and irrational forms"[38]. This modern 'man' then evolves into a primitive 'cave man':

> We have said that humanity (like Hamlet, my insertion, M.J.) is regressing into the *cave dwelling*, etc.–but he is regressing to it in an estranged, malignant form. The savage in his cave–a natural element which freely offers itself for his use and protection–feels himself no more a stranger, or rather feels as much at home as a *fish in water*. But the cellar dwelling of the poor man is a hostile element, "a dwelling which remains an alien power and only gives itself up to him insofar as he gives his blood and sweat"–a dwelling which he cannot regard as his own hearth–where he might at last exclaim: "Here I am at home"–but where instead finds in *someone else's* home, in the house of a *stranger* who always watches him and throws him out if he does not pay the rent[39].

To understand this very strange scene let us turn back to Marx's idea of the fetishism of commodities where products of the imagination have been reified as monstrous beings endowed with a life of their own. Let us then relate this with Freud on the mentally ill person. Now those versed with Freudo-Marxism will know that there is a similarity between Marx's critique of reified consciousness and Freud's idea of mental illness. In *The Uncanny* (*das Unheimlich*), Freud talks of the mental patient who fantasizes that life has been given to lifeless objects. He feels that some object that in reality is only an object has truly a life of its own. Here Freud's patient is filled by the feeling of dread.

In his analysis of the great literatures of the world, Freud asks why this process of thinking takes place. We will go into Freud in order that we understand why the parliamentary leftist fears the Revolution with a Revolution. Freud calls this the "uncanny". The uncanny according to Freud is "related to what is frightening–to what arouses dread and horror...It tends to coincide with what excites fear in general"[40]. There is an "unknown nature of the uncanny"[41]. Further the uncanny is "that class of the frightening which leads us back to what is known of old and long familiar"[42]. Freud explains the term "uncanny" in various languages. In Greek it implies the "strange" and "foreign", in English it means "uncomfortable", "uneasy", "gloomy", "dismal", "ghostly", "haunted", while in Arabic and Hebrew the uncanny means the same as "daemonic" and "gruesome"[43]. In opposition to this strange world of the dead which are given life is *Heimlich.* It indicates that which "belongs to the house", "not strange", "familiar", "tame", "intimate", "friendly", "well", "free from fear", "familiar", "amicable", etc.[44]. In *Unheimlich* the negative character is held: "eerie", "weird", "arousing gruesome fear", "ghostly", "motionless like a stone image", "secret and hidden", etc. Freud quotes Schelling, ""*Unheimlich" is the name of everything that ought to have remained...secret and hidden but has come to light*"[45].

The main theme linking Freud's analysis of the uncanny with Marx's estranged mind is found in Freud's statement, whether "an apparently animate being is really alive; or conversely, whether a lifeless object might not be in fact animate"[46]. And what happens in this realm of the lifeless object that appears endowed with life? The person becomes mentally estranged and is seized by the "phantom of horror"[47].

And it is here that we understand the politics of the parliamentary leftists. This horror of being estranged is also the horror of the complete loss of the self. In this realm of the loss, a process of doubling and duplication takes place. Consider how Marx's "cave", the "non-home" which becomes the "home" becomes the parliament where one has sought refuge. We knew that earlier, religion was the place where one sought refuge, now the parliament has become the religion in the age of late imperialism in permanent crisis.

Let us see Marx's dialectic at work. In Marx: there is through the process of self-alienation (*Selbstentfremdung*), whereby one has the "duplication (*Verdoppelung*) of the world" into an "imaginary world" and a "real (*weltliche*) one"[48]. We thus have two worlds: (1) real one: the world of the work place, the slums, the exploitation of workers, etc., and (2) the imaginary one: the world of the parliament. What we get is a "self-cleavage" (*Selbstzerrissenheit*) and "self-contradictoriness" (*Sichselbstwidersprechen*) in the heart of our Hamlet, the prince of revisionism. In this self-cleavage, the class structure of society detaches (*abhebt*) itself and establishes itself in the clouds as an "independent realm" (*selbständiges Reich*)[49] as the temple of parliamentary democracy. Hamlet takes the form of the *Doppelcharakter*[50], this lying schizophrenic double character, this double character, who he loses all sense of concrete reality, loses his real body and gets plagued by his imaginary-deluded mind.[51]

Hamlet's Schizophrenia and the Problem of the *Doppelcharakter*

This *Doppelcharakter*, this double character, is firstly the basis of Marx's analysis of the capitalist mode of production. Its poetic significance it finds in German Romantic poetry that grasps the essential trauma of alienated society. Temporarily Hamlet leaves us and Faust along with the devil Mephistopheles enters:

> Two souls alas do dwell within his breast
> each going apart from the other.[52]

When Goethe's *Faust* mentions the dialectical process of human consciousness: the conflict between good and evil, the finite and the infinite, temporality and eternity, suffering and ecstasy, he was bringing on to the front of human knowledge the question of the nature of existence, as well as the problem of the search for the transcendent world. Faust searches for some transcendent world, in almost the same way as Hamlet is trying to flee from both his reality as well as from his bout of insanity. Yet Goethe's search for this supersensible world is itself caught in a form of madness. Faust (Goethe's main character) has somehow obtained all knowledge of the world, and seized by the postmodern theme of the world of "ends", is also seized by the theme of the "end of knowledge". Yet he knows that there can be no "end", most certainly no "end of history", no "end of ideology", etc. And yet he knows that there is one "end" that he can never deny. He cannot deny the "end" of his own life. So he calls onto the devil and sells his soul in return for eternal youth.

Faust is seized by a form of false consciousness, almost by Marx's "mist enveloped regions of the religious world". He is seized by "the opium of the people"[53]. But Marx does not dismiss this experience as nonsensical. Because this experience is real human experience, based on real human suffering, he claims that it of great importance to understand it. And which is the most popular type of transcendent consciousness? Religion, so Marx says, is the "*inverted consciousness*" of an "*inverted world*"[54]. It is also:

> the general theory of this world, its encyclopedic compedium, its logic in popular form, its spiritual *point d'honneur*, its enthusiasm, its moral sanction, its solemn complement and its universal basis of consolation and justification. It is the fantastic realisation of the human essence (*phantastische Verwirklichung des menschlichen Wesens*) since the human essence has not acquired any true reality......
>
> *Religious* suffering is at the same time the *expression* of real suffering and a protest against real suffering. Religion is the sigh of the oppressed creature, the heart of the heartless world and the soul of soulless conditions. It is the *opium* of the people[55].

And it is the conflict of these two realms that haunt and taunt Hamlet, Faust and the parliamentary leftists that would occupy Marx. For him, the schism is formed not only in consciousness, but (to borrow the language of historical materialism) is found in the *base* itself. The duplication and the process of doubling takes place because something is rotten in the state of the economic base of capitalism itself. There is this form of schizophrenia that neither Hamlet, Faust, nor the parliamentary leftists can be cured of.

Let us try to understand how this type of schizophrenic tearing apart of the very being of radical politics has transfigured and reified one part of the left movement into revisionism. It has not understood that the parliament is no separate terrain alienated from class society, but like the state in general, is nothing but the committee of the entire bourgeois class. It cannot understand how the parliament has become the "rule of capital", and as the discourse of "dead substance" and as "past materialized and dead labour" becomes "a live monster that is fruitful and multiplies"[56]. It cannot understand this fruitful monster, that is also *transcendent* in character. As Marx says the commodity is essentially "transcendent"[57], where we have the process of disembodiment, or the *loss of the bodily form* of radical politics. After all parliamentary democracy speaks only in the "language of commodities"[58]. And in these language games the double as the *estranged other* becomes a "thing of terror"[59]. One part of the radical left has understood this, the other bows down before this "fantastic form (*phantastische Form*) that is completely different from reality"[60].

If Marx says that this alien world appears as "a very trivial thing", as well as "a very queer thing, abounding in metaphysical subtleties and theological niceties"; and because it is "transcendent" it "not only stands with its feet on the ground, but, in relation to all other commodities, it stands on its head, and evolves out of its wooden brain grotesque ideas, far more wonderful than "table turning" ever was"[61]; then he also means the same for parliamentary politics. The parliament, like capitalism, is a "complete mystification', because it is "the conversion (*Verdinglichung*) of social relations into things"[62]. We are no longer governed by humanity, but by monstrous things.

If all of us, governed by monopoly capitalism and the dictatorship of the totalitarian late capitalist state, are not completely at home in this estranged stage wherein marched the ghost of Monsieur Capital and Madame Rent, then at least all the supporters of the Indian state, from the Nehruvian liberals to the fascists, the Stalinists and the postmodern Fukuyamas celebrate this form of corporate totalitarianism, where what Marx calls "alienated thinking" and "thinking which abstracts from nature and real humanity, thus abstract thinking"[63] forms the dictatorship of monopoly capitalism and the complete colonization of the mind. Thus it is to this form of abstract thinking that attention must now turn.

Traditional Philosophy and the Etiology of the Ghost

We will now move into the terrain of historical materialism and redraft Marx's celebrated statement: the economic base determines the political and ideological superstructure as: *the reified base determines the estranged mind.* Reading the *Economic and Philosophic Manuscripts of 1844* in conjunction with *Capital* necessitates this conclusion. In this way we shall see how Marx understands, firstly the superstructure as the estranged mind, as well as the bourgeois base as endowed with a mind of its own. While we shall see the relation between philosophy and alienation, how philosophy is merely a false path, we shall also see how philosophy becomes necessarily an idealism (this is Hegel's thesis) and a form of disembodiment, mimicking the deep structure of the accumulation of capital. We have already seen that this idealism/disembodiment leads to a form of psychotic withdrawal from reality which in turn represses insurrection. The ghost enters, then exits, enters and then exits. The parliamentary leftist enters and exits, enters and then exits. The eternal recurrence of the neurotic becomes the eternal recurrence of the parliamentarian.

Since we are saying that there is a deep connection not only between alienation and the capitalist economy, not only between alienation and the state (that includes parliamentary politics), but also between alienation and traditional philosophy, we need to go into this analysis. We will see the double binding–Marx's thesis: the binding of alienation with capitalism and traditional philosophy and Lenin's binding of philosophical idealism with parliamentary cretinism. As we shall see the space that traditional philosophy and parliamentary politics occupies is *alien space* because their philosophies and politics are based on the metaphysics of the *estranged mind.* And it is to this estranged mind that philosophy must turn its attention. One goes thus into the realm of the unconscious. If Marx went into the dual sites of (1) the alienated political economy and class struggles that emanate thereon, along with (2) the study of the estranged mind; one needs a psychoanalytic revolution to proceed further to explicate Marx's great discoveries.

To study the deep structure of idealist philosophy we will begin with the case of disembodiment in *Capital*. We will find this strange loss of bodily form. This is the very basic principle of *Capital*: the economic base of commodity production, so Marx states, is devoid of any substance. It now exists in the form of a "ghostly reality" (*gespenstige Gegenständlichkeit*)[64]. Now this *ghostly base* is the "Being" (with a capital "B") of classical metaphysical thought (Heidegger is the culmination of this project of the "Destiny of Being"). This "B" with a capital "B" takes the form of God. In fact the first two pages of *Capital* indicate that there are three levels of this spectral being: "Being", "being", and "beings". The last (beings) as the life-world of real humanity is alienated, only to posit: "being" and "Being". From these, the first, i.e. "being" is understood as a reified relations of production and the second "Being" is what Marx calls the *Gemeinsame*[65], the "common something" between beings. And Marx declares this "something" as the ghostly reality, the world that is devoid of its concrete material character. In this way there is a "correspondence" between the occult texts of classical metaphysics and the context of the capitalist mode of production. The estranged and reified mind of Hamlet, so one states after Marx, is grounded, in the essence of capitalism itself. Marx concludes with the statement that just as all idealist philosophers were wrong in attributing an idealized character to reality, so too capitalism (in its very essence) idealizes and reifies reality.

There are two models of historical materialism developing therein. Firstly the classical one, as articulated by Marx in *The German Ideology* where the economic base (as the concrete unity of productive forces and relations of productions) is said to develop a superstructural consciousness; and the second model (from the thesis of disembodiment from *Capital*) where the base itself loses its material character and develops a *spectral mind* (from its lost body). We shall proceed to the second model. We saw already that the essence of this model is its "ghostly" character. It must be noted that the deep structure of capitalism is constituted of this "ghostly" form, while the surface structure is the "thingified" form (where human relations are converted into a relation between things).

Let us sum up this part, in order to understand the structure and function of this reified mind: the surface structure of capitalism, or the "thingified being" loses its bodily form, and in this process of disembodiment finds a purely "ideal or mental form"[66]. So what do we find? That the reified mind is found in the alien object (this is how the inanimate object is given life with a 'mind' of its own). This idealized or mental form Marx calls "value", and has two essential structures in it: (1) substance of value, i.e. abstract labour, and (2) magnitude of value, i.e. socially necessary labour time taken to produce the commodity. The combination of these two we call *abstract time.* Now this "ghostly reality" that we mentioned before is this abstract time–time existing independent of the human and natural world. Remember Marx's phrase: "Time is everything, man is nothing; he is, at the most, time's carcass"[67]. This estranged time is realized as the essential structure of capitalism. In political practice it is realized as the politics of "ripe time". This ripe time is Walter Benjamin's "homogeneous time" which gives way to "messianic time".

Now this deep structure of the "ghostly" form will develop a *phenomenal form*–or exchange value (which will develop further as money, capital, surplus value, profit, etc.). This phenomenal form is the symbolic life-world embedded in "hieroglyphic" language[68]. Just as the ancients wrote in mystical hieroglyphic language, so too the most modern of the moderns, the bourgeoisie inscribes their true reality in the anti-humanistic hieroglyphics of capital accumulation and profit making. We have pointed one location of the reified mind. But this consciousness is not only located in the ground-structure of bourgeois reality. It also has a second location—the location of the superstructure.

Now as humanity is trapped in the falsity of the ghostly world, it creates the "duplicated" world, the world of (what is known since Feuerbach as) the "projected lack" or simply "false consciousness". This is the second fetishized object created. This process Marxism calls "ideological", a process predicated necessarily on the *loss of the Real.* Ideology, in its very essence means the erasure of the Real.

So we come back to the theme of Freud's uncanny. One exists in the double worlds (base and superstructure) of the demonic unhomeliness. And in this demonic uncanny character of the world, Marx says, "My will does not possess, it is possessed"[69]. This is how we are able to understand Marx's statement on Hegel, where the (estranged and psychotic) world appears as "the Idea" and which is said to become the demiurge of all reality.

So while the idealists considered life as a sort of surrealist dream, Marx evokes history in order to awaken society from this opium-dictated nightmare. For it is in the radical character of history that the above mentioned "forms of consciousness" (*Gestalten des Bewusstsein*) are decoded as "forms of estrangement" (*Gestalten der Entfremdung*)[70]. History is not the history of the "Idea", but the histories of humanity. As estranged history it is represented in the realm of "consciousness", because "we detach the ideas of the ruling class", to borrow Marx's celebrated statement, "from the ruling class itself and attribute to them an independent existence....."[71]. That is why Marx claims that idealist philosophies and the ideologists talk of the "mystery", "fantasies", etc.[72]. On the contrary, the materialist conception of history is in direct anti-thesis to the ideological conception:

> It has not, like the idealist view of history, to look for a category in every period, but remains constantly on the real *ground* of

> history; it does not explain practice from the idea but explains the formation of ideas from material practice, and accordingly comes to the conclusion that all forms and products of consciousness cannot be dissolved by mental criticism, by resolution into "self-consciousness", or transformation into "apparitions", "spectres", "whimsies", etc., but only by the practical overthrow of the actual social relations which give rise to this idealist humbug; that not criticism but revolution is the driving force of history, also of religion, of philosophy and all other kinds of theory[73].

That is why Marx's conception of the "radical" always implies the essential being of humanity–the human essence (*das menschliche Wesen*). This human essence grasps things by the root. And for humanity the root is the human itself.[74]. Radical consciousness implies humanized consciousness, and as humanized consciousness goes through the process of de-alienation. It takes the dialectical notion of the *Aufhebung* and thus as "transcendence" literally sublates the whole history of philosophy by actively negating the mystical and speculative parts of this history, just as it actively negates the class character of hitherto existing histories. It thus ends the history of the "prehistory of human society"[75]. Communism is the emancipation of consciousness as also the emancipation of all the senses. It is the consequent realization of the human essence.

Archaeology of the "Mystical"

If indeed it has been thought so many times–from Lenin to Dunayevskaya and Kevin Anderson–that Hegel stands central to the world proletariat and that his dialectical method was a tremendous revolution in the history of philosophy. Indeed Hegel was (as the great nineteenth century Russian revolutionary Alexander Herzen had said) the "algebra of the revolution". It is thus to Hegel that we turn our attention. To understand both the revolution with a Revolution as well as understanding how the ghost comes in to destroy this revolution, one must understand how Marx involved a double reading of Hegel—of the rationality of Hegel that was enveloped in the phantasmagorical mist of the mystical shell. All Marxists know that there is a tremendous contradiction in Hegel and that only a very critical and revolutionary reading could qualify as a Marxist text.

To understand this we go to two more of Marx's sites that he discovers: (1) the mystical in Hegel and (2) the rational. The point that Marx raises, namely that there is an element of rationality in Hegel's philosophy, despite it being enveloped in mysticism has led many Marxists to decode the rational and mystical in Hegel. Since Engels' *Feuerbach and the End of Classical German Philosophy*, the 'dialectical method' was given the status of the revolutionary and the rational, while the 'system' was discarded as conservative and mystical. Unfortunately the point of the mystical in Hegel was not sufficiently analysed, since Engels' doctrinal statement on Hegel nor was it taken seriously by orthodox Marxism. It was left to thinkers following Lukács' *History and Class Consciousness*, namely Theodor Adorno, Lucio Colletti, Herbert Marcuse, etc., who claimed that the mysticism in Hegel was not something to be forgotten or banished from philosophical reasoning. The mysticism in Hegel was a serious philosophical issue for Marx, which he continuously probed into starting with the *Critique of Hegel's Doctrine of State* and culminating in *Capital*. Hegel's central thesis is that philosophy is an essential an idealism. This is what Hegel says in the *Science of Logic*: 'Every philosophy is essential idealism or at least has idealism for its principle, and the question then is only how far this principle is actually carried out.' Now this thesis of the hegemony of idealism is taken very seriously by Marx. This hegemony is not merely the counter-revolution of idealist philosophers, but something much more. What then is this 'something more' than the philosopher's idealist dream? Marx defines philosophy as the 'alienation of the human essence'. Consequently it is to this terrain of the estranged human essence whereby Marx articulates the history of class societies as being predicated on estrangement.

Though Hegelian-Marxist scholarship largely rests on the philosophical shoulders of the trio of Lukács, Gramsci and Karl Korsch, it was Lenin in the middle of the First Imperialist World War who went to reading Hegel's *Science of Logic* and then claiming that without understanding the entire Hegelian *Logic* it was impossible to understand even the first chapter of Marx's *Capital.* Later it was the American Marxist-Humanist Raya Dunayevskaya followed by Kevin Anderson who elaborated the radical importance of Hegelian logic for the construction of international revolution, especially on the theory of party, trade unions the imperialist war, rights of nations to self-determination, etc. This is what Anderson has to say:

> Certainly none of the major Marxist thinkers of the twentieth century who were also leaders of the parties–not only Leon Trotsky, Luxemburg, Karl Kautsky, or Mao Zedong–with the sole exception of Gramsci (and even then those writings were locked away in prison or in party archives for many years afterwards), had made that "return" to the Hegelian dialectic that Marx called "the source of all dialectic." Nor did any of the younger layer of Bolshevik theoreticians, such as Bukharin or Yevgeny Preobrazhensky, make such a move.[76]

It is from this space of revolutionary Leninist dialectics that we turn to the philosophical connection between Hegel and Marx. We begin with a question: *"Did Marx ever write a "phenomenology of the mind", a dramaturgy of Hamlet the Prince of parliamentary democracy and if he did so was Capital this phenomenology and dramaturgy?"* When Marx wrote to Engels in 1858 that he wanted to "make accessible to the ordinary intelligence–in two or three printers' sheets–what is *rational* in the method which Hegel had discovered but at the same time enveloped in mysticism"[77], and when this claim was reiterated in the 1873 'Afterword to the Second German Edition' of *Capital* Vol. I, when Marx wrote that Hegel made the dialectic stand on its head (*Sie steht bei ihm auf dem Kopf*)[78], and it was necessary to invert (*umstülpen*) him in order to discover the rational kernel within the mystical shell, he made possible, firstly a revolutionary reading of Hegel, and secondly, the history of philosophy itself. In this revolutionary reading Marx laid bare the possibilities of the emergence of a radical humanity freed as if from the chains of reified reason.

In the 1830s when the intellectual life of Europe was pondering on the legacy of Hegel's philosophy, Hegelianism was itself split into the warring camps of the Right (or Old) Hegelians–the pioneer being Carl Fredrich Göschel whose *Aphorismen über Nichtwissen und absolutes Wissen* immortalized the claims to onto-theologize Hegel by identifying the *Geist* with the Christian God, followed by von Henning, Hotho, Forster, Cornadi, Schaller and Marheineke; and the left Hegelians–of David Strauss, Bruno Bauer, Max Stirner, Moses Hess, Ludwig Feuerbach, Arnold Ruge, Karl Schmidt, Marx and Engels. It was since these Young Hegelians (especially Feuerbach's great philosophical revolution, defined as the *Umkehrungsmethode*) that the possibilities of a radical appropriation of the Hegelian methodology was sought. But it was "Engels' time honoured distinction" to borrow Louis Althusser's phrase[79], that was drawn in *Feuerbach and the End of Classical German Philosophy*[80], between the conservative mystical system of Hegel and the radical and rational method that would not only draw the line of demarcation between the mystical and the rational but also the philosophies of idealism and materialism. While this distinction would form on the one hand the new understanding of the history of philosophy and the possibilities of the creation of a revolutionary humanism, it would also form the crux of orthodox Marxism, especially the 'orthodoxy' of the Second Internationalism that would convert this distinction into a doctrinal dogma. Georgoi Plekhanov (the alleged 'father' of Russian Marxism) would embody this dogma. (Lenin's *Philosophical Notebooks*, in contrast to metaphysical materialism, criticizes this form of contemplative philosophizing. What revolutionaries need is the activist conception of consciousness, and the consequent praxical type of theorization. When Lenin observed in *What is to be Done?* that without revolutionary theory there can be no revolution, he was advocating the philosophy of praxis). In contrast to this praxis inspired school, one knows how the above stated dogmatic misreading of Engels would crystallize not only in the philosophy of the Second International as Menshevik fatalism but would also culminate in Stalin's counterrevolutionary coup against revolutionary Marxism. The return of the repressed would not spare even the revolutionaries.

One thus contextualizes the case of Hamlet's estrangement and relates this case of estrangement with Marx's analysis of consciousness within the critical genealogy of estrangement. It relates philosophical consciousness (as exemplified both in Hegelian thought as well as the general history of philosophy) with the problem of estranged thought. It then relates the question of the reified mind with the process of alienation (*Economic and Philosophic Manuscripts of 1844*) and disembodiment (*Capital*), on the one hand, and that of ideology defined as "false consciousness", on the other hand. It consequently inquires into the possibilities of a post-reified consciousness. Revolutionary Marxism deals not only with the production of this post-reified consciousness, it deals with the creation of a humanized, universal, classless society, a society which is essentially about real thinking people.

We have already seen that Marx's philosophy is not a continuation of traditional philosophy. We already saw the *Aufhebung* (transcendence) of philosophy[81]. In this character of the *aufheben*, Marx poses the question of philosophy. Philosophy, so the young Marx had announced, is not some great wisdom seeking enterprise. Instead it is to be understood as:

> nothing but religion rendered into thought and expounded thought, i.e. another form and manner of existence of the estrangement of the human essence (*Form und Daseinsweise der Entfremdung des menschlichen Wesens*); hence equally to be condemned.[82]

And as Marx never bothered to pose or solve questions in the abstract onto-theological world of traditional philosophy, he insisted on a paradigm shift into a new realm–the realm of living humanity, or what he calls the human essence. One cannot pose questions in the phantasmagoria of the traditional philosophical world. In fact questions posed in this fantastic world are the questions posed by the reified mind, the estranged and deranged mind of class stratified societies. So what is this "reform of consciousness", a reform that he demanded right from his doctoral studies on ancient Greek philosophy[83]? In 1843 Marx wrote to Arnold Ruge:

> The reform of consciousness consists only in making the world aware of its own consciousness, in awakening it out from its dream of itself, in explaining to it the meaning of its own actions. Our whole object can only be–as it is the case in Feuerbach's criticism of religion–to give religious and philosophical questions the form corresponding to man who can become conscious of himself. Hence our motto must be: reform of consciousness not through dogmas, but by analysing the mystical consciousness that is unintelligible to itself, whether it manifests itself in religious or a political form. It will then be evident that the world has long dreamed of possessing something of which it has only to be conscious in order to possess it in reality.[84]

It is here that we shall connect Lenin's celebrated 'philosophic laughter' ("philosophy is only a lost path") with Marx's theory of philosophy as the alienated mind. Now we know that at least since the *Economic and Philosophic Manuscripts of 1844* philosophy as the "estranged mind" (*entfremdete Geist*)[85] was related as "estranged form" (*entfremdeten Form*)[86] to estranged reality itself. Philosophy would be considered as estranged significations of a distorted and class-based reified reality itself. The manner of understanding philosophy and human civilizations would henceforth involve a radical break. Marxist philosophy has consequently be defined as the critique of the genealogy of estrangement. One must remember that the texts explicitly dealing with the question of alienation, *Contribution to the Critique of Hegel's Doctrine of State* and the *Economic and Philosophical Manuscripts of 1844* would emerge on the scene of world philosophy only in the late 1920s and the early 1930s when they were published by David Ryzanov. These texts were completely unknown to an entire generation of revolutionary Marxists. Thus the early generation of Marxists, Karl Kautsky, Plekhanov, Rosa Luxemburg, Lenin and Trotsky, did not know of these works. From these, Plekhanov and Kautsky would render a form of contemplative materialism (which would be inherited by the Stalin school of falsification), whilst Lenin, Trotsky and Luxemburg would embody the praxis school of revolutionary Marxism. Probably the greatest blunder, created by the 'contemplationists' would be the formation of the "copy theory" in Marxist epistemology–the theory that states that the "mind" is only a "copy" of an objective reality that functions independent of the mind. The estranged mind would re-enter the corridors of philosophy, but this time disguised in the clothes of (revisionist) Marxism.

So what did Marx do with the burning questions of philosophy? Does Marxism pose the questions of an "objective reality"? If so, is this objective reality, to be understood as being "independent of the mind"? Or is the mind to be understood as a part of objective reality? Why should one separate the "mind" from "objective reality"? Would not the question of seeking an "objective reality independent of the mind" be nothing but rephrasing the issue of a reality that is estranged from humanity? Would not these traditional questions of philosophy consequently be nothing but the reflection and expression of estranged, capitalist society itself?

When Marx talked of relating Hegel to the problem of the mystical and the estranged mind, he was also using Hegel as an exemplar to critique the history of class societies itself, where the question of idealism was related to the problem of the bourgeois mode of production and the capitalist state. Remember that when Marx is talking of the importance of understanding Hegel, he is relating Hegel as the already defined "alienation of the human essence" in the *Economic and Philosophical Manuscripts of 1844* and also to the question of "value" of bourgeois political economy, in *Capital*[87]. He thus relates the mystical with the problem of value–"and even here and there, in the chapter of value", Marx claims to have, "coquetted with the modes of expression peculiar to him"[88]. Marx in the same paragraph talks of the "mystification" in Hegel, indicating the relation of bourgeois political economy with the problem of the mystical[89], just as in the early *Contribution to the Critique of Hegel's Doctrine of State* he related the "mystical" with the ontological inversion performed by metaphysical philosophy–i.e. where the subject and object, existence and essence, the real and the imaginary, civil society and the state are inverted. In "speculative philosophy", so the young Marx had once announced, reality appears in "the reverse (*umgekehrt*)"[90] *Reality appears not as itself, but as another reality*[91]. What then is this if not estranged reality or the lost paths of reified reason that Lenin would laugh at?

Philosophy and the Problem of the Reified Mind

To get back to our original question as to why the Revolution with a Revolution has been forgotten, let us go back to Marx's classical question: "Why does humanity appear "upside down" or literally "standing on its head" (*auf den Kopf gestellt erscheinen*)?"[92] And just as Lukács had gone to quite another problematic, the problematic of the reification of consciousness, we go to the question of the "upside down world", the world that devours Hamlet.

Here we shall be able to articulate our anti-Althusserean character of reading Hegel. Contrary to Althusser, we are claiming that this concept of inversion, is not a metaphor, as thought by the anti-Hegelian philosophical school[93], but a scientific category (*Begriff*) that explains the precise nature of Marx's problematic itself. Firstly, one has to consider the streams of the ideas of inversion in Marx's works. To proceed into the question of philosophy as well as the dominant ideologies of class histories as the inverted mind, Marx claims that an *Aufhebung und Verwirklichung der Philosophie* (transcendence and realization of philosophy) is necessary[94]. But what is this *Aufhebung* and why did Marx use this apparently Hegelian term? What did Marx and Hegel mean by this?

Principally *Aufhebung* implies (we noted this very briefly in the beginning) a "lifting up", in which there is a transcendence, which *preserves* as well as *abolishes* reality at a *higher* level of being. For Hegel, *Aufhebung* "has a twofold meaning....on the one hand it means to preserve, to maintain, and equally it also means to cause to cease, to put an end to. Even "to preserve" includes a negative element, namely, that something is removed from its immediacy and so from an existence which is open to external influences, in order to preserve it"[95]. For Marx there are multiple *aufheben*. In *On the Jewish Question* he proclaims an "*Aufhebung* of religion"[96], and an "*aufzuheben* of these real distinctions"[97], while in the *Contribution to the Critique of Hegel's Philosophy of*

Right. Introduction Marx reiterates the "*Aufhebung* of religion as the (abolition) of the illusory happiness of the people"[98]. In the *Economic and Philosophic Manuscripts of 1844* Marx proclaims the "positive *Aufhebung* of all estrangement"[99], followed by the "transcendence of all classes" (*Aufhebung aller Klassen*)[100] along with the explosive "*Aufhebung* of the basis" itself[101]. This principle of the complete transcendence of estrangement with the *Aufhebung* of private property (*Aufhebung des Privateigentums*) and the state (*Aufhebung des Staates*)[102] remains the *condition sine qua non* of revolutionary Marxism. Humanity has itself to be understood as perpetual transcendences.[103]

To contextualize the question of the reified mind, to understand how the reification of not only consciousness, but the reification of humanity's very being and consequently the reification of political praxis takes place, let us concretely understand the *very physical space* of this reification and how the transcendence of this reification can take place. This is the central dialectic in Marx: where there is "the estrangement of the human essence" (*die Entfremdung des menschliche Wesens*) and "the transcendence of this estrangement" (*die Aufhebung des Entfremdung*) which is also understood as "the appropriation of the human essence" (*die Aneignung des menschliche Wesens*)[104]. Get back this human essence is to get it back in terms of a political praxis, the praxis of the Revolution with the Revolution.

The point now in the theory and praxis of perpetual transcendences is to locate when in history, estrangement emerged, and if philosophy is to be understood as the estrangement of the human essence, then when in history did the reified mind appear? In which philosophical systems was this estrangement represented? Was there a class struggle in the realms of estrangement and philosophy? Should one understand the foundational systems of Greek philosophy, initiated by Anaximander of Miletus (c. 610-546 BC), author of the lost treatise *On Nature* who introduced the concept of *arché* ("the primary principle" or beginning of all things), Thales of Miletus (c. 624-547 BC), Anaximenes of Miletus (c. 588-525 BC), Anaxogoras of Clazomanea (c. 500-428 BC), Pythagoras of Samos (c. 580-500 BC), the alleged 'student' of Zarathushtra, followed by the legendary Socrates (469-399 BC), Democritus of Abdera (c. 460-370 BC), Plato (428-348 BC), Aristotle (364-322 BC) and then culminating in Epicurus (341-270 BC), as a straightforward "love of wisdom", or the "estrangement of the human essence"? Or is there a combination of both wisdom as well as estrangement, making it a 'love of estrangement'? Or is there a struggle between these two?

How does one seriously understand Marx's statement of philosophy to be understood as the estrangement of the human essence? Or would philosophy include not only the estrangement of humanity, but also its appropriation? In fact it is the latter theme that interested Marx: philosophy as estrangement has to go through the *Aufhebung* in order that a true and human-based consciousness can make its appearance. That is why Marx disagreed with the Hegelian essentialisms of converting the world into the "Idea". The world is the world of humanity and sensuous nature. There can be no consciousness existing in the alienated form of the "Idea". So in anti-thesis to estrangement, Marx says that, "consciousness [*das Bewusstseins*] can never be anything else than conscious being [*das bewusste Sein*] and the being of men [*das Sein der Menschen*] in their actual life process"[105]. There can never be any *rational* free floating consciousness. (There can however be an *irrational* free floating phantasmagoric mind posed as the estranged mind.) Consciousness is always embedded in the world, whether in rational or irrational forms. That is why Marx says that it is life (*Leben*) that determines (*bestimmte*) consciousness[106]. This theme would haunt the entire life span of Marx's life: "It is not the consciousness of men that determines their existence, but inversely (*umgekehrt*), their social existence that determines their consciousness"[107]. But what does speculative philosophy do? It remains is the bosom of the heavens producing illusory phantoms. It soars to heavens blue:

Kant and Fichte soar to heavens blue
Seeking for some distant land,
I but seek to grasp profound and true
That which–in the street I find[108].

This metaphor of the street, the roaming wanderers and the *flâneur* of Walter Benjamin belongs to this world, even if the streets are littered by the transcendent, irrational, psychotic commodities. We know that this theme of the street is far removed from Hamlet's castle that is engulfed by dark shadows and darker ghosts. We know that this was a theme that continuously occupied Marx and Engels (just as it occupied the minds of the French materialists in particular and the history of materialism in general) as also Freud's critique of mental illness, Adorno, Benjamin, the surrealists and the modernists. So both the philosophical as well as the aesthetical modernists (whether the revolutionary Marxists, the avant-garde cubists or the impressionists) would operate in this *worlding of the world*. Marx's insistence with the worldliness of consciousness (even as the estranged mind), was on the one hand the epistemological basis of his dialectical materialism, as well as the political critique of commodity production, the state and the hegemony of private property and estrangement. Remember Marx's dictum: *alienation creates private* property[109]. Alienation not only creates private property, the state and human repression, it also creates the reified mind. So this theme of the conflict of human estrangement and the critique of estrangement, of the alienated human essence and the struggle to appropriate this human essence remains central for Marx's studies on consciousness.

The "mind", so once Marx declared, is cursed and burdened with "matter"[110]. The theme that consciousness is always predicated on social being–a definite Feuerbachian theme would form the crux of revolutionary Marxism:

> The production of ideas, of conceptions, of consciousness is at first directly interwoven with the material intercourse of men–the language of real life. Conceiving, thinking, the mental intercourse of men at this stage still appear as the direct efflux of their material behaviour. The same applies to mental production as expressed in the language of the politics, laws, morality, religion, metaphysics, etc., of a people. Men are the producers of their conceptions, ideas, etc. that is, real active men, as they are conditioned by a definite development of their productive forces and of the intercourse corresponding to these, up to its furthest forms.....If in all ideology men and their relations appear upside down as in a *camera obscura*, this phenomenon arises just as much from their historical life-process as the inversion of objects on the retina does from their physical life-process........ The phantoms formed in the brains of men are also, necessarily, sublimates of their material life-process, which is empirically verifiable and bound to their material premises. Morality, religion, metaphysics, and all the rest of ideology as well as the forms of consciousness corresponding to these, thus no longer retain the semblance of independence. They have no history, no development; but men developing their material production and their material intercourse, alter, along with this their actual world, also their thinking and the products of their thinking[111].

In *The German Ideology,* Marx makes a distinction between a "self-sufficient philosophy" (as the estranged mind) and the scientific description of reality[112]. Let us now relate this self-sufficient philosophy as the estranged mind with the reading of the history of philosophy as the *Aufhebung* of philosophy. For Marx, this combination of the already mentioned *Aufhebung* and *Verwirklichung* implies a "lifting up" (the first "moment" in the dialectics of the *Aufhebung*) from the reified conditions of estrangement, whereby as the realization of philosophy, the Real that was hidden in the misty regions of the Imaginary and the Symbolic, appears. Now this appearance of the Real is the radical moment in the history of humanity. The history of philosophy will be the continuous games that involve the concealment and the revelation of the Real. But what is this "Real"? And how does this alleged borrowing of Lacan's terms be able to shed light on Marx's philosophical revolution? What does Marx do with the entire edifice of the history of philosophy, and why did Marx insist on going through the history of philosophy? Consider Marx: *One cannot turn one's back on philosophy and mutter a few irritable and banal phrases over its* shoulder[113]. One has to go through these lost paths, one has to go through this estranged human essence. It is "necessary to study", as Althusser once quoted Lenin, "the falsest of all false paths (*der Holzweg der Holzwege*)"[114]. Dialectical materialism is the "*theory of philosophy as a false path*"[115]. And this study requires the most radical solution: *the negation (Negation) of philosophy, i.e. philosophy as* philosophy[116]. In the *Theses on Feuerbach*, Marx proceeds into the epistemological mechanisms of philosophy. Philosophy as expressed in the binary oppositions of materialism and idealism, emerges when the human essence as the radical subject of the labouring being-in-the-world is itself fragmented into the binary forms of subject and object. The resultant schools of thought: idealism and materialism are the "false consciousness" expressed therein. Materialism, so Marx claims, which includes the darling of the radical Young Hegelians, Feuerbach himself, conceives reality only in the form of object (*Form des Objekts*) and the binary opposite of contemplation (*Anschauung*)[117]. It does not grasp the activist character of radical humanity, it cannot grasp revolutionary praxis. It can only understand theory as "the only genuinely human attitude"[118]. Note how this same metaphysics that Marx critiqued would emerge in the

Marxist movement itself. Why is this so? What did Marxism of the Second International do? It created an estranged signifier called "Matter". The entire human history is conceived as the teleological evolution of "Matter". In this teleology one cannot talk of consciousness and will. Thus there is no consciousness, no will in this metaphysics of matter. One should remember the counterrevolutionary impact of this metaphysics of matter in the international proletariat movement. While this metaphysic was constructed by the "father of Russian Marxism", Plekhanov, it was the 'children', Stalin and company who converted this metaphysic into an onto-theology. The classical text of Stalin's *Economic Problems of Socialism in the USSR* proclaimed the greatness of the "laws of history" existing "independently of human will". The will was enslaved to these theological "laws". Stalin's summary was human consciousness exists only as a Platonic 'mirror' to the reified and personified "laws" working independently of humanity (remember Plato's Ideas?). Mao in response called Stalin a metaphysician (a highly derogatory term in Marxism). Stalin (himself trained as a priest) of course could not conceive of revolutionary Marxism. This error of a "Matter" devoid of humanity, was pontificated by Stalin as a "science". The chief error was that all materialists (Feuerbach included, as the *Theses on Feuerbach* went) wrote their grand philosophies in the text of reality existing in the "form of the (estranged) object". Remember how Gramsci would critique this metaphysics as mechanical materialism and fatalism, and also how Lukács would call this episteme an "inverted Platonism". Remember also how this object (in the "form of the *object*"), or "thing" (*Ding*) becomes the *personified thing* in Marx's theory of alienation and reification.

On the other hand, so Marx announced, the idealists seized the activist conception, but "only abstractly", since, "idealism does not have real sensuous activity as such"[119]. So what form of activity does idealism know of? Phantasmagorical activity. And what is this phantasmagoric activity? It is a form of activity constituted within a world where there is "absolutely no connexion with their physical properties and with the material relations arising there form"[120]. And why is there "absolutely no connexion" with the physical and material life-worlds? Because we have now a reality posited which appears in "fantastic form (*die phantasmagorische Form*) of a relation between things (*Verhältnisses von Dingen annimmt*).[121]

We need to conclude by saying that in societies based on commodity production, a *fetishism of the mind* takes place, a process where humanity is estranged, and where life is conferred to the inanimate object. We have already noted the relation of the "form of the *object*" and the already mentioned "independent beings" who are "endowed with life", strange beings that would frighten not only Hamlet, but also Stalin and the parliamentary democrats.

And so after Stalin poured the holy water of socialism onto the commodity declaring that now commodity production is socialized–thus creating the tale of 'socialist commodity production'–his loyal followers struck by the fetishism of the mind and magical powers being bestowed onto inanimate objects, deserted the streets and pleaded to the liberals and democrats in the parliament not to pass the holy American sponsored nuclear and other corporate imperialist bills. They thought that they would enter parliament, and just as Gandhi would appeal to the conscience of the fascists to convert to a more non-violent form of fascism, the parliamentary leftists thought that they would convert all Indians (if not the whole world) to the good religion of parliamentary socialism. They forgot Marx's statement, "in the history of civilization the conscious element plays a part so subordinate."[122] They also forgot Freud on the unconsciousness, Marx on the political unconscious, and the estranged mind which are so intrinsically bound to the capitalist mode of production in particular as well as the history of class societies in general. Something is strange in the state of class societies whereby Hamlet's estranging reason refuses to leave the scene of world history.

On Historical Materialism as a Rigours Science

As we shall see the politics of the Revolution with the Revolution will remain at the basis of this discovery of the case of alienated Hamlet. History, as we shall know it, is very unlike Althusser's anti-humanist "history without the subject". And because there is the 'subject' always at the basis of Marxism, and because Hamlet is not one case in the phase of humanity, but perpetually around, one has to go more into the details of the relation between Marx's science and his dramaturgy that he penned in *Capital.* In almost every way science (for Marxism) has been in anti-thesis to both scienticism as well as to utopia. One knows that though Marxism, by and large, has been almost contemptuous of the word "utopia", at least Ernst Bloc had tried to rehabilitate utopia in his magnum opus *Principle of Hope.* Yet Marx's revolutionary communism stands clearly against the dimensions of utopia. Marx is most certainly interested in Hamlet, how he gives up the revolutionary path to be in a state of perpetual mourning. But his interest in Hamlet is not as a utopian, but as a dramatist. In the *Communist Manifesto*, Marx and Engels talked of the somewhat 'critical' thinking of the Utopian Communists, but a critique that was tied down by its own metaphysics, a metaphysics that did not want to get involved in the politics of class struggle, but in fact wanted to preach class reconciliation.[123] They violently opposed the independent political action of the proletariat and transfigured politics in the "blind belief in the new gospel".[124] Their founders were revolutionaries; their followers were founders of reactionary sects.[125] Consider Marx:

> The significance of Critical-Utopian socialism and Communism bears an inverse relation to historical development. In proportion as the modern class struggle develops and takes definite shape, this fantastic standing apart from the contest, these fantastic attacks on it, lose all practical value and all theoretical justification. Therefore, although the originators of these systems were, in many respects, revolutionary, their disciples have, in every case, formed mere reactionary sects. They hold fast be the original views of their masters, in opposition to the progressive historical development of the proletariat. They, therefore, endeavour, and that consistently, to deaden the class struggle and to reconcile class antagonisms. They still dream of experimental realization of their social utopias, of founding "*phalansteres*," of establishing "Home Colonies," of setting up a "Little Icaria"–duodecimo editions of the New Jerusalem–and to realize all these castles in the air, they are compelled to appeal to the feelings and purses of the bourgeois.[126]

And that is why I will continue to talk of science. Not only is utopia standing the dimensions of science, as we know it has been the theological right-wing that has always had contempt for science. And yet it is this same theological rightists that have cursed and dammed science, it is the same who have always been ready to go for the most bourgeois methods. In this sense there is form of 'rationality', in this form anti-reason, a form of rationality that we call instrumental reason. Take the case of the conservative Islamic regime of Iran and how they look at this. It is Davari-Ardakini the philosopher-ideologist of the reactionary Islamic Republic of Iran and mentor of Mahmoud Ahmadinejad and said that modern science is tied down to humanism. Trained in Heideggearean metaphysics he critiques technology as a form of departure from primordial Being. Consider this case of anti-science:

> Notwithstanding the roots of Westoxication in Greek philosophy and its 2500 years of history, its specific and predominant form has emerged with the Renaissance. With the appearance of

> Westoxication, the old form of history is abolished and a new man is born who is no longer submissive to the *Haqq*. (*Haqq* here in the present Iranian sense is primordial Being in the Heideggerean sense, or to be precise, *estranged and despotic Being*. It ought not to be confused with the Sufi usage of *Haqq* (as 'truth', 'right', 'authentic'). My insertion. M.J.). He forgets the *Haqq* so that he can replace Him to expropriate the earth and the heavens.......The freedom of religious beliefs in the Declaration of Human Rights means alienation from religion; it means leaving the individuals to their own devices so that they may do whatever they want with religion in their private lives and have any religion they want... Modern man sees his own image in the mirror of *Haqq* and instead of entering into a covenant with *Haqq*, has entered into a covenant with himself. Therefore it is inevitable and natural that such a man would turn his back to religion and cover up his act with claims to nationalism, internationalism, liberalism, collectivism and individualism.[127]

It is from this critical conjuncture that I now insert the Marxist idea of historical materialism as the location of the Real of the Revolution. On the one hand it is totally against the Heideggerean idea of primordial Being. Science, in the very Marxist sense, is literally *Wissenschaft* or knowledge seen in a holistic-dialectical manner. Very obviously it is empirical knowledge as distinct from idealist constructs. One needs material reality to operate, or as Lacan had said one has to put the "real object" at the centre of discourse. In this sense one has to insist that Galileo's physics serves as a paradigm shift in the history of the sciences. His telescope showed that it was not belief that stood at the horizon of human knowledge, but intellect. Modern sciences were thus born, not merely as one form of knowledge, not only as the European sciences, as not only as Edmund Husserl once suggested, but as also goes on a Eurocentric celebration of its own narcissistic self. We thus take science as an objective and universal method. Since Bacon and Galileo there can be no going back. Galileo showed the cosmos freed from onto-theology and the original sin. One had to do the same with human reality.

It is keeping this theme in mind and relating science with critical humanism that I go into the deliberations of the Marxist concept of science. Despite my disagreement with the entire Althusser inspired school, I am compelled to say that probably the best metaphor to explain Marxism as a rigorous science comes from Althusser. In *Lenin and Philosophy*, he talks of Marx discovering a new continent of knowledge, the continent of history, that follows the two prior continents discovered: mathematics and physics.[128] Since "continents" signify imperialism and not knowledge, one may have to say that Marx discovered a new galaxy. So let us say that Marx discovered a new galaxy and constituted a new discipline: historical materialism. One may like to have the term "new galaxy", for imperialism has not yet colonized outer space, despite their great efforts. But one will also like to use this term since Marx uses the metaphor of the telescope to indicate how he has discovered this new site of human understanding[129].

Since for Marx, science is not bourgeois science, not the methodology that tears humanity from concerns of knowledge, it is best to understand that for Marx science is what he himself called "human natural science", where human concerns are what he calls 'natural', i.e. which takes all reality as a collected whole or as a living as 'species'. Remember that he talks of the science of species being (a term that he uses following Ludwig Feuerbach). What happens in this perceptive of science is that it humanizes all knowledge, because it keeps the real corporeal human being with its essential powers at the basis of science. Despite this process of humanization, let it be known that rigour is always present in demonstrating his point.

So how does one reconcile the questions of scientific rigour and radical praxis? Can praxis be directly synthesized with a form of what we know as determinism? Or are they completely unrelated? To answer this it is necessary to move from the real of Anglo-American philosophizing that we in India are so used to and move to the terrain of Classical German Philosophy. It is necessary to understand that Marxism is not a determinism governed by the rule of the march-past of history that is governed by the fiction of the "iron laws of history". And since Marx does (so it seems at the level of appearance, at least in the 1867 Preface to the first edition of *Capital*, Vol. I) talk of the "natural laws of capitalist production" that work with "iron necessity towards inevitable results" it is necessary to say that this master translation done by Samuel Moore and Edward Aveling under Engels' direction and supervision is highly faulty. Marx instead talks of "*eherner Notwendigkeit wirkenden*" where capitalism works, or knits, or even weaves with "brazen necessity"[130]. Secondly, the term "inevitable" (or *unvermeidliche*) is not used by Marx (which the English translation shows). Marx never talks of an "inevitable revolution" "that is freee from revolutionary praxis. Marx instead talks of "*durchsetzenden tendenzen*" or "forceful tendencies". There is it seems the force or compulsion of (and in) history. Thirdly, it must be noted that when Marx used the term "determination" (*Bestimmung*) in his celebrated theorem: the economic base determines the political and ideological superstructure, this term *Bestimmung* ought not to be read as "formation" where the economic base forms a superstructure.

Now when Marx had introduced the base-superstructure model in his theory of historical materialism, he also inscribed several other models within it. One could differentiate these models as the pure model and the models existing in chaotic form. The model apparently appearing the most at the manifest level of Marx's texts (as well as in the theories and praxis of revolutionary of Marxism) is the pure form model. (We are using the term "pure form" from his *Theories of Surplus Value*, Part I,[131] and the term "chaos" or "chaotic whole" from the *Grundrisse*[132]). By "pure form", Marx means that phenomenon occurs in "typical form", "most free from disturbing influence"[133]. But never in the real world does history function solely in manner of this building like metaphor. Engels' late letter states this problem[134]. The base and the superstructure work in the dynamic relations of dialectical chaos, the economic base stated to be the determining element in the *last resort.*

The whole problem lies when one is not able to understand the deep structures of his scientific revolution. What this science of historical materialism does is that as rigorous science it makes a difference between two sites: (1) what one calls after Marx the model that appears in "pure form", and (2) the chaotic model. The pure form model is the model that functions at the deep level of scientific inquiry. It operates at the level of everyday life-world in an altogether different way. I call this way of the appearance of the pure form, the chaotic form.

Consequently Marx's theory of history is rigorous, especially his main thesis on the historicity of capitalism and the inability of capitalism to function when its forces of production have transcended the social structure of society, or in other words, transcended its relations of production. This thesis claims (made famous by Marx in his 'Preface' to his 1859 *A Contribution to the Critique of Political Economy*) that within the base, there occurs a clash between the two levels of the base, i.e. between the forces and relations of production, where the latter become fetters to the development of the productive forces, thus creating havoc in society. Since a clash occurs between the two, one witnesses the transformation in the social structure. In this deep structure, or the pure form, Marx discovers three sites: (1) forces of production (the level of the sciences and technologies), (2) production relations (the structure of society which are comprised of the ownership of means of production and the class struggle), and (3) the ideological superstructure. The former two are the "base" while the third rests on this base. Since quite often there has been a tendency to have a reductionist explanation which gives priority to only the first site (Cohen's explanation in his magnum opus *Karl Marx's Theory of History* is one good example), one must make it clear that the pure form lays only a certain methodological guidelines for understanding this new science. In this pure form we see that the movement of level 1 (forces of production) to the level of say "A" witnesses the likewise movement of level 2 (relations of production) to "A". When level 1 becomes "A^1", then level 2 likewise follows the same. This, as we insist, operates at the pure form, or the cell form. It is found in the laboratory of historical materialism. Its mode of appearance in the everyday life-world takes an altogether different form. One therefore has to differentiate the cell form from the body form. This cell form is a "typical form that is free from disturbing influences".[135] Now when one says that there is an inexorable to move from site 1 to site 2 this is an afterthought, or a scientific thought that operates in the cell form.

The pure form of science shows what Marx calls the "progressive development" of history from primitive communism, via the Asiatic societies, European slave society, feudalism, capitalism, and the consequent struggle for communism. Since there has been a sort of misunderstanding whether Marx implied a unilinear theory of history (made sacrosanct by Stalin) and since Marx's *Ethnological Notebooks* (where he talks of non-European societies and their own concrete course of historical development) has almost been ignored, it must be stated that Marx did not impose a teleological view of history where only the forces of production were seen to determine the development of the course of history. One only has to note Marx's 1877 letter on the Narodniki misinterpretation of history, where he differentiates the concrete analysis of primitive accumulation of capital in Western Europe and the European transition from feudalism to capitalism from what he calls an imposition of this theory onto the whole world, where one has the fantasy of "an historico-philosophico theory of the general development prescribed by fate of all nations".[136] One cannot have, as Marx notes, a "master key" as a "general historico-philosophical theory", for what in the end happens, is being supra-historical.[137]

History, and Marx's account of it, is dynamic and fluid and cannot be kept in the magical jar where the predetermination of theological theories are substituted by some sort of 'science'. Marxism is not this born-again theology, nor is it the phantasmagorical gin kept in the magical jar. One must here not only bring to attention Gramsci's reading of theology parading as Marxist 'science', but also those of Walter Benjamin. That this theory came into being at the time of the revisionism of the Second International (which did not want to fight for the revolution, but wanted it to 'inevitable' happen, and because it did not 'inevitable' or 'magically' happen one had to support the necessities of so-called history including imperialist wars) is well known. That it was made sacrosanct by the Stalinist counterrevolution should also be noted because the Stalinist bureaucratic state capitalist *new class* wanted to justify their counterrevolution. Stalin's last work *Economic Problems of Socialism in the USSR* is an example of this parading of theology as science where he redrafts theology's "laws" and humanity's necessary obedience to these "laws" as a "science".

What one sees, is what one calls after Marx, a "so-called science" which works in a "roundabout way".[138] We call this a *'duplicate' science* because it seems to imitate the scientific method, while in actuality it mimes it in an altogether manipulative way. It is not what one calls "reason" but what we call after the Frankfurt School's use as an "instrumental reason". It uses the "authority of science" while in actuality invoking "magical formulae".[139] This duplicate scientist attempts to be a utopian, but in actuality becomes a *duplicate utopian*.

This duplicate utopian does talk of miracles and miraculous solutions. But this duplicate can never talk of the very basic questions: *"What is humanity?"* and *"How is free humanity possible?"* Consequently if it was said that philosophy is always linked with the sciences[140], then one also says that the sciences (the science of the material world) are inexorably linked with philosophy. The world is thus linked to the question: *"How is free humanity possible?"* So if one says that the space that is opened that of the real object as the material for investigation, one now says that science and philosophy are placed under the genre of "critique". What this Marxist science does is places itself as a "critique", a point that not only covers the original Kantian concern of the analysis of the conditions of knowledge, but primarily deals with the analysis of human emancipation. Marxist science deals thus with human emancipation. It becomes "scientific dialectics" as Marx called it, that is derived "from a critical knowledge of the historical movement which itself produces the material conditions of emancipation".[141]

In contrast to this reading of Marxism as a science, there is another site usually opened by the reactionary ruling classes: that of the anti-sciences that appear as what Marx chided as "apparitions", "spectres", "whimsies" and other types of idealist humbug[142]. One has to stress this site because the ruling classes love exploring this site–from the RSS and the Jamaat-e-Dawa to the American culture industry. While one wants a "Hindu nation", another wants the "Islamic caliphate". The Americans of course who desire the end of the world (one only has to watch American satellite TV), which is another pop form of their biblical nonsense could be said to be the biggest producers of the factories of the "apparitions", "spectres" and "whimsies".

Now one knows that these are being bombed not only in Libya and Afghanistan, but also in Indian universities, under the label of "ancient Indian wisdom". Scientific temper has not only to confront these apparitions in the age of late imperialism in permanent crisis, it will have to wage a just war of independence. In case India has to remain a secular and democratic society, this scientific revolution has to be the mainstay of the Indian public intellectuals. One only has to see the philosophy departments in India, and one will find the exact parallel that goes on in Pakistan. Obscurantism and superstition govern the South Asian feudo-bourgeois imagination. But there is another space that is different from both these of the sciences and the organized superstitions. This space is the space called utopia. Engels' *Socialism: Utopian and Scientific* sharply divided science from utopia. Science had the essential moments of description, explanation and prediction based on verifiable material principles, while utopia is a mere longing for an apparent just or even sometimes a classless society but based more on metaphysical sermons than on material practice. Science occupies a *verifiable space*, utopia occupies an *alien space*.

Since Marx calls his science a *human natural science*[143], and since this vocabulary is by and large forgotten, one needs to conceptualize this very idea, for it is this idea that resolves the contradictions and tensions between the social and the natural sciences. It is also this idea that opens a new framework where not only is this human natural science as *dialectical and historical-humanist materialism* found its method of operation, but also how the humanization of the sciences is rendered possible. If we saw that historical materialism as articulated in Marx's 1859 Preface to *A Contribution to the Critique of Political Economy* articulates the three basic structures of human history in its "pure form" or "cell form": forces of production, production relations and the political and ideological superstructure; the problematic of human natural science from the *Economic and Philosophic Manuscripts of 1844* activates the dialectics of the natural sciences and philosophy in the genre of "humanity's essential powers"[144]. The ontology of humanity, or human *Dasein*, that articulates the sciences as springing from "human sensuous essential powers"[145] becomes the new basis for the understanding of Marx's new galaxy of knowledge. Humanity thus stands at the base of Marx's scientific revolution. The question of seeing history as a "process without a subject" (as done by Althusser) is a fallacy that stems from his reading of Marxism as "theoretical anti-humanism". One must recall Marx here: "Humanity is the immediate object of natural science..."[146]

What Marx does is that he radically transforms the ideas of subjectivity and objectivity thus being able to articulate anew the idea of science and philosophy. Nature is thus no longer to be seen as an objectivity lying "out there", independently of human existence. Nor is subjectivity to be seen as dealing with merely 'consciousness', the 'will', etc. Instead one deals with subjectivity and objectivity as forms of human praxes and thus as a "manifestation of human reality".[147] It is class society (and capitalism in particular) that erases human reality and fragments the diverse systems of knowledge. If there was to be a sense of unity between the natural sciences and philosophy it would only be what Marx calls a "momentary unity" that is based on a "chimerical illusion"[148]. "The will was there", as Marx says, "but the power was lacking".[149] This is how Marx comprehends the complex dialectic and also articulates the possibilities of a real unity between philosophy and science:

> The natural sciences have developed an enormous activity and have accumulated an ever-growing mass of material. Philosophy, however has remained just as alien to them as they remain to philosophy. Their momentary unity was only a chimerical illusion. The will was there but the power was

> lacking. Historiography itself pays regard to natural science only occasionally, as a factor of enlightenment, utility and of some special great discoveries. But natural science has invaded and transformed human life all the more *practically* through the medium of industry; and has prepared human emancipation, although its immediate effect had to be the furthering and the dehumanization of humanity. Industry is the actual, historical relationship of nature, and therefore of natural science to humanity. If, therefore, industry is conceived as the *exoteric* revelation of humanity's *essential powers*, we also gain an understanding of the *human* essence of nature or the *natural* essence of humanity. In consequence natural sciences will lose its abstract material–or rather, its idealist tendency, and will become the basis of *human* science, as it has already become–albeit in an estranged form–the basis of actual human life, and to assume *one* basis for life and a different basis for *science* is as a matter of course a lie.[150]

Remember, as the above passage goes, Marx's main concern is human emancipation. Recall again that Marx talks of estrangement in this text and the struggle against this estrangement. This struggle is in no way an 'inevitable' struggle. It is real struggle, where Lacan's real comes once more on the scene of the Real of the Revolution. And that is why one states that Marx's idea of science is not the positivist searching of laws that are independent of humanity. Instead it keeps the Feuerbachian concern for sense-perception that is said to be the basis for all science.[151] There are four main points that one can draft as Marx's fundamental understanding of the natural sciences: (1) articulating humanity's essential powers, (2) of understanding the genesis of nature and human society, (3) articulating sense perception in the twofold forms of sensuous consciousness and sensuous need, and (4) of understanding *humanity as humanity* and human history as part of natural history.[152] Marx thus concludes: "History itself is a *real* part of *natural history*–of nature developing into humanity. Natural science will in time incorporate into the science of humanity, just as the science of humanity will incorporate into itself natural science: there will be *one* science".[153] Thus by putting the Feuerbachian idea of human essential powers and the Hegelian idea of truth as a process[154], Marx transcends the sites of human estrangement and the consequent emergence of what he calls "pseudo questions", and comes onto the new site of *humanity as radical historization*. Marx's science thus becomes the science of human knowing as well as human emancipation. If "knowing" and "being" are no longer considered as opposites, then "knowing" and "emancipation" are also not regarded as binaries. To transcend this state of binaries is the fundamental point for the scientific revolution. Once one does this, then science becomes a material force and literally "grips the masses"[155].

On Hegel

We saw when we were discussing the cases of both traditional philosophy and Hamlet that in mystified form the Hegelian revolution becomes a "fashion" because it transfigures and glorifies the existing state of things, while in its rational form it is a scandal and adomination to bourgeoisdom.[156] So what is this Hegelian fashion, this mystification that glorifies the inglorious; and how can one transform this fashion into a scandal that rattles the doctrinaire professors?

The answer at first glance seems to be rather simple. One has to understand the dialectic as the algebra of the revolution. Hegel is this algebra. One has to understand it. To understand Marx's newly discovered continent/galaxy one needs to briefly understand the differences that Hegel made between the sites of the understanding (*Verstand*) and reason (*Vernunft*). To put it very simply, *Verstand* is the domain of the formal sciences governed by Aristotlean logic (with its dualisms that was perfected by Kant), while *Vernunft* is the new domain that Hegel discovers, the domain of post-Aristotlean logic. Now we know that Marxists of the last century put this Hegelian discovery at the centre of their discourse. We know of Illyenkov's *Dialectical Logic* and Zeleny's *Logic of Marx*. We know that Lenin in 1914 and following him Lukács and Gramsci, followed by Raya Dunayevskaya, one time colleague Trotsky, and founder of Marxist-Humanism, placed the Hegelian logic at the centre of revolutionary Marxism.

However at second glance the dialectic between the mystical and the rational is much more complex. At least since Engels' *Feuerbach and the End of Classical German Philosophy* the rational was said to be the dialectical method, while the mystical was written as the Hegelian metaphysical system. But what Engels did not clarify was the relation between the Hegelian "mystical" and the phenomenology of the estranged commodity that Marx outlined in *Capital*. The "mystical" is not to be understood as merely the idealist gibberish that university professors churn out, or what the media industry continuously propagates. Then what is Marx's understanding of the Hegelian mystical? What Marx means is that the mystical is that which is predicated to the mode of thought that accedes to the mode of thinking that mimes the phenomenology of the commodity that Marx outlines in the theory of value in *Capital*.

Now what Marx does is that he follows the genealogy of the commodity. He studies how it is a de-humanized process, that it is estranged from humanity, and after this first estrangement, it loses its material character to take an idealized form of value and exchange-value. Marx thus contextualizes the Hegelian mystical. He grounds it in capitalism and the phenomenology of the commodity. So estrangement, value and exchange-value do not allow Hegel to fully revolutionize his system. Hegel remains in what Marx calls "the orbit of estrangement".[157] And yet there is the rational that Marx accepts, a rational that Lenin in 1914 with the commencement of the First Imperialist World War (and the betrayal of the Second International to the forces of social imperialism) thought it necessary to read the entire *Logic* of Hegel. This what Marx says about Hegel:

> The outstanding achievement of Hegel's *Phänomenologie* and of its final outcome, the dialectic of negativity as the moving and generating principle, is thus first that Hegel conceives the self-creation of humanity as a process, conceives objectification as loss of the object, as alienation and as transcendence of this alienation; that he thus grasps the essence of *labour* and comprehends objective humanity–true, because real humanity–as the outcome of humanity's *own labour*. The *real, active* orientation of humanity to itself as a species-being, or his manifestation as a real species-being (i.e. as a human being), is only possible if he really brings out all his *species-powers*–something which in turn is only possible through the cooperative action of all of humankind, only as the result of history–and treats these powers as objects: and this, to begin with, is again only possible in the form of estrangement.[158]

So one reads Hegel not only in the dual sites of the rational and the mystical, but also understands the "one-sidedness and limitations" of Hegel[159]. What Marx did was take this logic and discover a New Physics by not applying the dialectical method onto reality, but discovering the mechanisms of world history as they actually function. What marks what we call the rigour of the scientific method is its unconditional materialistic method, or as we may dare to say, the dialectical materialist method. But this science is not merely a study of so-called "objective facts". It is humanist, or if one may say after Gramsci it is historicist and humanist, or better still one may say after Marx that it is "naturalism and humanism" that is distinct from both materialism and idealism, and yet it unifies the truths of both[160]. Marx's materialism is not to be confused with traditional materialism. Or to go further, it involves what the young Marx called, a human natural science which is also the natural science of humanity.[161] And since it is this humanism with passion realized as the "essential power of humanity energetically bent on its object"[162], which is said to be the basis of Marxist science, I had earlier christened it an "irresistible science".[163]

We saw above that Hegel breaks out from the domain of the understanding, the domain that the Frankfurt School had called the domain of science as *power seeking*, as different from reason (*Vernunft*) which is the critical science of human emancipation. Now what we see is that this "irresistible science" is the dispeller of the phantasmagoria that comes in the way of critical and emancipatory thinking. This is what I talk of the irresistible character of Marxist science, an irresistibility that transforms the burning fire of theory into radical praxis. To transform the burning fire of theory into material praxis is to think once again of the Revolution with the Revolution. One firstly has to think of universal solidarity, and thus contrary to the postmodernists, think of the universal and the universal good that is realized in the real explosion of freedom and the sublime moment of universal solidarity where everything is rendered possible[164].

But if the *Real of the Revolution with the Revolution* appears on the scene of history, the "Unreal" as the *Counterrevolution with a Counterrevolution* also appears. And it is this Unreal-Surreal character appearing sometimes as the Iranian Ayatollahs, sometimes as the Muslim Brotherhood, sometimes as the RSS, that somehow compels us to look at this.

A Note on the Asiatic Mode of Production

Quite often according to bourgeois imagination, Marx is made to appear as, if not a Semitic prophet, then at least as a European fellow traveller of Hegel and a Eurocentric thinker par excellence. It is said that his theory of Asiatic mode of production and of oriental despotism, was a European invention.

It is also said that one should not critique capitalism and imperialism but "Western civilization" (Gandhi's *Hind Swaraj* is an example) or even critique "Western Reason". It is thus said that the spectre of "Western Reason" is haunting the world. But in the end, not only is this ghost of Western Reason shown to be a false ghost, but the entire theory of "Western Reason" and its alleged critique is shown to be entirely fallacious. There is nothing really called "Western Reason". It lies only in the cranium of the imperialists and their right-wing accomplices. After all, not only would the RSS and the so-called "Islamic radicals", claim that there is something wrong with this rather strange creature called "Western Reason", but one also has academic industries based on this critique. One does not merely have to go to the works of Ashis Nandy and company to comprehend how this bad and awful "Western Reason" has harmed "Eastern Reason". One may also go to a number of the departments of the social sciences in Indian universities to see how they have literally "banned" this awful "Western Reason", only to welcome not merely the writers of anti-secular manifestos, but also Yoga and other spiritual and occult 'sciences'. That these same Yogis hail nuclear weapons and hail American imperialism, should not go unrecognized. That there is a distinct ideological bias one must note. Marx is the villain, Marx the European fellow traveller, Marx who apparently hated Asia. Consider Nandy for this type of ideological reasoning:

> Everyone knows, for instance, that Karl Marx thought Asiatic and African societies to be ahistorical. Few know that he considered Latin Europe, and under its influence the whole of South America, to be ahistorical, too. Johan Galtung once told me that he had found, from the correspondence of Marx and Engels, that they considered all Slavic cultures to be ahistorical and the Scandinavians to be no better. If I remember Galtung correctly, one of them also added, somewhat gratuitously, that the Scandinavians could be nothing but ahistorical, given that they bathed infrequently and drank too much. After banishing so many races and cultures from the realm of history, the great

> revolutionary was left with only a few who lived in history–Germany, where he was born, Britain, where he spent much of his later life, and the Low Countries through which, one presumes, he travelled from Germany to England.[165]

One needs to point out (contra Nandy) that even what is known as the 'beginnings of Western Reason' grew from a very close interaction between the Mesopotamians, Babylonians, Persians, Greeks, the Medes, Egyptians, Indians, etc., and that Greek philosophy did not emerge only from the womb of the Greek cranium. Clearly Heidegger was wrong in postulating the beginning of Western philosophy as a purely Greco affair that did not interact with other philosophies. What we now know (and this is what has been recently pointed out by Peter Hudis in his essay on Marx and the Muslims[166]) that European rationalism was directly influenced by al-Farabi, Ibn Sina, and Averroes, that Descartes was inspired by al-Ghazzali, and that al-Sijistani influenced dialectical thinking. One should also not forget Hegel's reference of the Sufi mystic Rumi in his *Phenomenology of Mind*. Human history is not understood as the 'Destiny of Being from the European stand point'. Instead one should talk of the *humanization of history* from what Samir Amin had talked of, namely, the three waves of *universalizing humanity* starting with the Persians, Chinese and Greeks that culminated in Judaic, Christian and Islamic thought (this is the first wave: the idealist wave) which then proceeded in the European Renaissance (the second wave) and then finally ended in Marxism[167]. When Marx talked of communism as being a synthesis of humanism and naturalism, he did not mean that the human was to be solely the European.

So for one thing there can be nothing really called "Western Reason" because there is nothing really called the "West" and the "East". Yet, and because, one has to see the dangers of this line of thinking that does not want to comprehend imperialism, but instead claim how "Western Reason" has destroyed Indian life (not to forget how it has destroyed the Iranian mullahs' lives, besides the lives of other transcendental fascists), one will have to go through these rather rough waters. Now we know that according to a certain line of thinking, we live in the grips of Western Reason. We shall now stick to the seriousness of this discourse.

Nativism of this sort (the CSDS in India, for instance) tied down to its binary half, Eurocentrism, it must be emphasized, are serious issues, not to be confused with mere academics, but directly with imperialism. We know that it is not merely the primordial nativist along with the Eurocentric thinker, but also American foreign policy that postulates a deep abyss between the 'West' and the 'East', or to be precise the North Bloc of capitalist nations at the centre of capital accumulation and the South Bloc of the nations of the periphery. I had earlier said that for Eurocentrism, the *West* is rational, while the *Rest* are said to be not mere mystics, esoteric thinkers, seekers of the netherworld and gymnosophists, but at least since 9/11 as simply barbarians.[168] The geo-political map of Eurocentrism, turned Colonial Reason, turned American foreign policy marching not only with the UN, the World Bank and the IMF, but primarily with the NATO looks like this:

> Until the last thirty years of the nineteenth century, everything to the east of an imaginary line drawn somewhere between Greece and Turkey was called the Orient. As a designation made in Europe, 'the orient' for many centuries represented a special mentality, as in the phrase 'the Oriental mind,' and also a set of special cultural, political, and even racial characteristics..... But mainly the Orient represented a kind of indiscriminate generality for Europe, as associated not only with differences and otherness, but with the vast spaces, the undifferentiated masses of mostly coloured people, and the romance, exotic locales, and mystery of 'the marvels of the East'.[169]

But Eurocentrism has been radically transformed from the days of William Jones and Thomas Macaulay. It is no longer the case that James Mill matters in constructing the imaginary of imperialism. Now we also have the Asian conservatives joining the imperialists to reframe the map of imperialism. What matters now is Samuel Huntington, with the Asian conservatives walking hand in hand. The 'East' is no longer exotic and marvellous. It is dangerous. The 'marvels of the East' has now been replaced by the 'war on terror'. 'The romance of the Orient' has been replaced 'by the problems of dealing with the Orient'.[170] Eurocentrism is no longer a benign ideology. It is imperialist state policy. Presently this new wave of dealing with the Orient is only another wave of primitive accumulation of capital and the re-working of Colonial Reason. At least since the last two decades the West has labelled this project as the project of globalization. The discourse of Orientalism has metamorphosized as globalization. Unlike the ahistoricism evident in Edward Said's *Orientalism* that sees Eurocentrism rooted in 'Western Reason' since Aeschylus's *The Persians*[171], we are situating Eurocentric discourses in the processes of colonization of Asia, Africa and South America. The underlying essence is the same–imperialism.

We turn to both Eurocentric thinking and its binary opposite, the view of the 'nativist' (the mimic of Eurocentrism). For both: non-European societies are homogeneous devoid of internal differences and contradictions. For both, India is 'Hindu society', mystical and tolerant. Hinduism existed since time immemorial, even before the Judaic god, Jehovah created the world. To this mythical view largely dominated by the discourses of certain types of Orientalism–from Anquetil-Duperron, William Jones, Charles Wilkins and Henry Thomas Colebrooke to the German Orientalism of Friedrich Schlegel and Maurice Winternitz–one inserts another discourse, the discourse of what I call the 'Indian

Fanonists', the radical democrats, who at least since the 1870s, reinterpreted Indian history from a radically new and different perspective, the radical secularist perspective of *non-Hindu history*. This very important re-working of the ideology of history started with the thinker and activist from Maharashtra, the Western part of India, Jyotiba Phule (1827-1890) and culminated with B.R. Ambedkar (1891-1956) for whom:

> Hindu society is a myth....Hindu society as such does not exist. It is only a collection of castes...A caste has no feeling that it is affiliated to other castes except when there is a Hindu-Muslim riot. On all other occasions each caste endeavours to segregate itself and distinguish itself from other castes. ....Indeed the ideal Hindu must be like a rat living in his own hole refusing to have contact with others. There is an utter lack among the Hindus of what the sociologists call 'consciousness of kind'. There is no Hindu consciousness of kind. In every Hindu the consciousness that exists is the consciousness of his caste. That is the reason why the Hindus cannot be considered to form a society or nation.[172]

The main passage that angers the neo-Hindu is the following one from Marx who postulated:

> ....idyllic village communities, inoffensive though they may appear have always been the solid foundation of Oriental Despotism, that they had restrained the human mind within the smallest compass, making it the unresisting tool of superstition, enslaving it beneath traditional rules, depriving it of all grandeur and historical energies. We must not forget that the barbarian egotism which, concentrating on some miserable piece of land, had quietly witnessed the ruin of empires, the perpetuation of unspeakable cruelties, the massacre of the population of large towns, with no other consideration bestowed upon them than on natural events, itself the helpless prey of any aggressor who deigned to notice it at all. We must not forget that this undignified, stagnatory, and vegetative life, that this passive sort of existence evoked on the one part, in contradistinction, wild,

> aimless, unbounded forces of destruction and rendered murder itself a religious rite in Hindustan. We must not forget that these little communities were contaminated by caste and slavery, that they subjugated man to external circumstances, that they transformed a self developing social state into never changing natural destiny, and thus brought about a brutalizing worship of nature, exhibiting its degradation in the fact that man, the sovereign of nature, fell down on his knees in adoration of Hanuman the monkey, and Sabbala, the cow.[173]

The fact that these 'offensive' passages of Marx correspond to those of Phule and Ambedkar seems to be forgotten. One here can recall Aijaz Ahmad who had said that "Marx's denunciation of pre-colonial society in India is no more stringent than his denunciation of Europe's own feudal past, or of the Absolutist monarchies, or of the German burghers; his essays on Germany are every bit nasty".[174] Ahmad's important contribution is that he presents Marx as visualizing the power of the caste system in the Indian village–"restraining the human mind within the smallest compass...." that equals his critique of "the idiocy of rural life" in feudal Europe.[175] Further, for Ahmad, Marx "regarded the caste system as an altogether inhuman one–a 'diabolical contrivance to suppress and enslave humanity', as Ambedkar put it in the preface to *The Untouchables*–that degrades and saps the Indian peasantry, not to speak of the 'untouchable' menial castes".[176] Reading Ahmad puts the criticism of Marx as a Eurocentric thinker on the mat. Ahmad reminds us of Marx's pertinent question: 'Can mankind fulfil its destiny without a fundamental revolution in the social state of Asia?'[177] One must state that Marx was no cultural imperialist and most certainly no follower of Eurocentric mode of reasoning who fantasized that all Asian people were unchangeable in character. Instead when one reads Marx on non-European societies as a critic of the dominant social groups, then one is able to read Marx on pre-capitalist, non-European societies in a more enlightened manner. The discourse on pre-capitalism cannot be reduced to the discourses of European feudalism. A clear-cut line of demarcation must be drawn between the caste-based village communities (which Marx abhorred, and which were romanticized by Gandhi) and the classless communes (which Marx supported). Remember that in the 1881 letter to the then Narodniki (and later revolutionary fellow traveller of Lenin in his *Iskra* days before moving to the Menshevik political position), Vera Zasulich, Marx talked of the vitality of primitive societies, a form of vitality that even modern societies lacked[178].

It is in this space that one understands how Marx's thesis is extremely different from the Eurocentric perspective and that Marx's reading of the Asiatic mode cannot be reduced to the imagination of Orientalism. For Marx there is nothing exotic or mysterious in the so-called 'Eastern' world. If anything is mystical (rather "magical and necromantic", if one recalls the chapter on commodity fetishism), then it is the West European bourgeoisie who are charmed by the fetishism of commodities and are constantly under the spell of money-making. As we know in the famous chapter on the fetishism of commodities in *Capital*, he says that the same market-driven European bourgeoisie are like the seekers of the souls of the people long dead, obsessed with the alienated and transcendent world of commodities, which "evolves out of its wooden brain grotesque ideas", as Marx once famously said, which is "far more wonderful than "table-turning" ever was"[179]. "Table-turning, as we all very well know, was the rage with the nineteenth century European aristocracy who actually sought to evoke the spirits of the dead. Mary Shelley's master piece *Frankenstein* was one such instance that noted the obsession of the bourgeoisie with the mystical and the dead. Thus when Marx talks of the capitalist class as necromantic magicians[180], he is not talking of something that is contingent to the capitalist class, but something that is necessary. Once we note this, we will also be able to note that Marx did not borrow the categories of

Orientalism, in fact, placed the very same placard of the eternal mystics on the unfortunate chest of the European ruling classes. It is at this site that one will be able to critique Edward Said's thesis of Marx as an Orientalist thinker.

Understanding thus that the fictitious exotic paradise is not to be found in the 'East', but in the world market, we can proceed further on the theorization of history. The Asiatic mode springs from the following theorization. According to this form of dialectical reasoning, the dissolution of the ancient communes did not give way to slave society–a form of reasoning that is present in Engels' *Origins of Family, Private Property and the State*–but to multiple class-based societies form the Greco-Roman ones to the Germanic, Slavic, Asian, American, African, etc. Consequently there was nothing *inherent* in history, per se, that led to only one form of historical development.

And since the ideas of the Asiatic mode of production and the Oriental state themselves have a history of their own; one will have to briefly visit this little history. One will have to note that Marx's ideas do not have to be forced into the political discourses of Aristotle, Machiavelli, Jean Bodin, Francis Bacon and Thomas Hobbes. For one, Marx, unlike the above thinkers, was not seeped in the imagination of Asiaphobia. He did not hold Asian societies in general to be despotic, without any history, or if not having a history then at least devoid of a sense of history. One will have to read Marx's articulation of "the unchangeableness of Asiatic societies" in a different context, not in the context of a hypostasized 'Asian culture' but in the concrete context of caste. For Marx, Asiatic despotism is directly related to the caste question and the nature of power emanating thereon, both the power at the village level, as well as political power that resided in the infamous Oriental despotic state. Caste, as Marx puts it, is not only the "solid foundation for Asiatic despotism" but also of its legendary stagnation[181]. Two features emerge: Marx does not generalize on Asia as despotic and stagnant, but claims that the caste element served for this very same stagnation and despotism. Secondly, in India, one does not talk of feudal landed property–thus no feudalism in India–but caste at the level of "completely independent", "idyllic republics" as well as the level of government. One cannot graft the concept of serf on the idea of caste, nor reduce the caste equation to the landlord/serf relation. Pre-capitalist relations of production in Western Europe and India would be totally different.

Science as Critique

To understand this line of thinking on so-called "Western Reason" that was perfected by thinkers as diverse from Gandhi to Adorno, Horkheimer and Heidegger that culminated in Michel Foucault it must be stated that there are two dominant strands of the discourse "Western Reason": one stressed by Edmund Husserl (and taken over by the Frankfurt School), the other being articulated by Martin Heidegger. In the first articulation, Western Reason begins with the Greeks and is built on the idea of rationality. It culminates in the modern sciences, to be precise technological reason, the domain that Hegel called *Verstand* (understanding). *Verstand* is strictly speaking not reason (*Vernunft*). The second strand of Western Reason is the Heideggerean one, again beginning with the Greeks and this time not culminating in the modern sciences, but in mythopoetics, to be precise European fascism that would, as Heidegger claim, rescue Western *Dasein* from the dangers of Bolshevism.[182] While the first stream of Western Reason ends in the modern sciences, the second one culminates in mythopoetics. There is it seems, a peculiar type of telos, almost a form of an iron law, what Heidegger called the "destiny of Being" which governs both these strands of Reason. We do not exist in the West. Yet we are gripped by this double edge of Western Reason.

And in this response to the double effect of Western Reason we take up the critique of the doubling effects of Western Reason (primarily the humanist critique of the crisis of the modern sciences) based on Marx's reflections on the relation between reason, the sciences and society. Along with this discovery–called the science of Marxism: historical materialism–we have the philosophy of Marxism: the critique of the estranged mind. The former asks the question: *"how is history possible?"*, while the latter asks: *"how is humanity (as emancipated humanity) possible?"* It is in this question: How is history-humanity possible?: that the critique of estranged reason finds concrete articulation.

We conclude with Marx's views on the specific understanding of the sciences. For Marx just as with Hegel's *Phenomenology of Mind* truth lies in the whole. Yet Marx's holism is distinct from Hegel's idealist holism. And this nature of dialectical materialist holism Marx outlines in his theory of the sciences whereby he distinguishes himself from both metaphysics as well as the technological rationalists. Now according to Marx, science is not merely a technological enterprise–a will to mere knowing, but a project towards human emancipation–a will to human freedom. Marx consequently claims that the scientific enterprise cannot be reduced to an estranged mind studying a reified nature, nor the control of nature by this estranged mind. The double will to knowing and human freedom cannot become a will to power. The very idea of calculation and control (that is at the base of the bourgeois understanding and practice of the sciences) have to be expunged from the scientific enterprise.

But besides emphasizing the idea of human emancipation as the core issue of the sciences, Marx also involves a radical critique of the intervention of the capitalist division of labour (and this ideology of the bourgeois misunderstanding of the sciences) into the sciences. One does not have to unconsciously give consent to the fragmentation of the sciences that capitalism drives them to. Instead one has to de-alienate the sciences from this ghettoization of knowledge, that bourgeois ideology (under the pretext of knowledge) under Corporate Imperialism strives for. One has to argue of a coherent science–a non-schizophrenic science. Marx uses the term "one science", a "single science" (or a unified science)–a science of history with its "two (inseparable) sides": of the history of nature and the history of humanity.[183]

So what Marx does is differentiate the science of emancipation–the historical materialism of understanding humanity as a unified species–the humanist natural sciences from the ideology of the sciences, and thus distinguish the essence from the appearance. The former keeps the humanist and naturalist concern central to its philosophical repertoire, while the latter actively negates it. Marx thus keeps both humanity at large and nature in general at the centre of his scientific concern. Marx is thus both a humanist and an environmentalist. What we have in the Marxist landscape is the incorporation of the "science of humanity" (*Wissenschaft vom Menschen*) into the natural sciences.[184] This new science–historical materialism–is now known as "*human* natural science" which is at the same time a "*natural science of humanity*"[185]. Historical materialism is not about "iron laws" governing humanity and nature; it is about humanity and nature. We now have the humanization of nature and the naturalization of humanity.[186] The biblical-bourgeois spirit of anti-naturalism and anti-humanism has to be exorcised.

Yet Marx claims that leaving the natural sciences (which in fact is the realization of the labour of *Gattungswesen*)[187] to the spontaneous activity of capital accumulation renders it not only metaphysical and theological but also psychotic and barbaric. Both the natural sciences and the philosophical project governed by the capitalist division of labour turn a blind eye to one another.[188] They are the two Faustian souls tearing off the breast of humanity. The "human essence of nature" (*das menschliche Wesen der Natur*) is divorced from the "natural essence of humanity" (*das natürliche Wesen des Menschen*).[189] And in this great gap between nature and humanity, between the natural sciences and the human sciences, the crisis of the modern sciences first emerged, a crisis that is inexorably woven to the crisis of capital accumulation. And thus one insists that the problem cannot be posed as the mere crisis of the sciences, but the crisis of the capitalist project itself. Not only do society with its warring classes and their infinite ideologies but also science now appears in "estranged form" (*entfremdete Gestalt*).[190] It is at this site that Marx asks: how is "a genuine, comprehensive and *real* science" possible?[191] So if the natural sciences have slumbered into a reified state claiming to have life of its own, and sometimes even taking on the role of theology that it itself had removed from the centre state of world history, then one may say that one needs to psychoanalyze the sciences—one needs to understand its political unconscious, in order to humanize it.

Now besides Marx's dialectical and historical materialist thesis on scientific holism—human-natural sciences as radical emancipation—there is also the dualist understanding of the sciences, which did not understand the historicity of the scientific method. On one end of the critique of the modern sciences was Husserl who claimed that the European sciences had lost their basic humanist concern and on the other end of the spectrum was Horkheimer's and Adorno's *Dialectic of Enlightenment* which castigated not only the sciences but the entire project of Western Reason as the tyrannical development from Odysseus to Hitler. It seemed thus that fascism and imperialism were culminating moments of Western Reason with the modern sciences seeming to mediate between the ancient Greeks and fascism.

But to understand the history of the problem of the crisis of the sciences one has to understand that the problem is deeply rooted in the neo-Kantianism of the Heidelberg Circle. According to this type of thinking, especially Dilthey, there is a difference between explanation (*Erklären*) which functions in the natural sciences and understanding (*Verstehen*) which operates in the social sciences. The latter studies subjective meanings of historical actors, a realm totally missing in the natural sciences. It would thus be a fallacy (according to them) to mime the natural sciences and to raise it to an exemplary status. The natural science (according to the neo-Kantians) studies laws independent of human subjects, the human sciences studies not merely human subjects, but their consciousness, will, etc. But there is another dominant feature which is present in the debate in the methodology of the sciences, a feature that was raised by Georg Lukács in *History and Class Consciousness* and Husserl in *The Crisis in the European Sciences and Transcendental Phenomenology.* While these two texts are rigorously different, there is a shared theme—the concern of the loss of the humanist structure of Reason, and the claim that the rise of the modern sciences is responsible for this loss, besides the third claim that the modern sciences have itself an unexamined base which leads to an irrationality. But if the principle theme is the critique of positivism (in the 1894 Rectorial address Wilhelm Widelbland had initiated the critique) the dualism of the neo-Kantian method gave no possibility for a humanist solution. Lukács, as the heir to this Kantian dualism, would transform the idealist dualism of Kant to Hegelian idealism. Remember Lukács was the youngest and latest member of the Heidelberg Circle, who after a period of romantic anti-capitalism typical of the late nineteenth and early twentieth century anarchist thought, drawing inspirations from thinkers as diverse as Nietzsche, Kierkegaard, Dostoevsky and Sorel, would by 1917 shift to an ultra-left form of Hegelian Marxism.

For Lukács, Marxism is not a type of a 'science' modelled after the natural sciences, as much as it is a type of a radical act.

For him all 'scientific' mimesis are fallacious, and Marxism, if it attempts to model itself after the natural sciences, would collapse into a quietism, typical of the positivist school of thought. In this sense not only would Karl Kautsky and Plekhanov be mistaken in creating a theology of the natural-scientific school of thought, but also Engels himself was to blame for constructing the 'dialectics of nature', the chief fault with this thesis being that it leaves out the fundamental thesis of Marx–revolutionary praxis.[192] Not only would this alleged 'science' relapse into an ideology, but would become a metaphysic itself.[193] The main problem (as we noted earlier) is that it would have an uncritical and unexamined base that would stand outside the 'scientific' process itself.

But the main fallacy of the natural sciences, for Lukács (he should have said "the ideology of the natural sciences" or "the spontaneous philosophy of the natural scientists") is that it studies supra-historical laws, and thus relapses into a metaphysic of the eternal laws of nature. If history is suspended, then so is the project of revolution. Marxism consequently collapses. There are five points within this argument: (1) loss of totality within the natural scientific model of explanation, (2) rationalized objectivism, (3) pure quantification, (4) the reification of facts, and (5) abstract formalism. For Lukács, none of the above can operate as Marxism. But the chief fallacy is the alleged anti-historical nature of the natural sciences, besides the also alleged theme of the *iron laws* of nature, where humanity is converted into a tool of this *inevitably occurring phenomena* in nature. Fatalism is the main principle of the natural sciences. When one talks of necessity, repetition and prediction in the sciences, then life is said to be governed by these apparent fatal laws of nature. Science becomes theology. And humanity has to rebel. Anything other than rebellion is folly. If one has to rebel against God to become a humanist, then now one has to rebel against both the natural sciences–and also against nature itself. The Romanticism in this critique is evident. But then *History and Class Consciousness* would become a sort of a New Age Bible. For the natural sciences (as well as nature) are not only estrangements, but literally the Biblical 'Fall' itself–in Lukács's words: "a charnel-house of long-dead interiorities".[194] 'Man' is condemned not to freedom, but to the reification of the eternal recurrence of estranged nature. 'Man' is only matter pure and simple (as Lukács would read the philosophy of the natural sciences). Consequently materialism becomes an "inverted Platonism.[195] All scientists are Platonists in the reverse. It is only the soul (Lukács's understanding of the proletariat) that would rebel against this naturalized-reification of humanity.

This thesis would be in a way both utopian and radical, radical in the sense that it would challenge, if not the very basis of the legitimating of capitalist societies, then at least its instrumental reason–the modern-bourgeois sciences themselves. The modern sciences (one should say: "the bourgeois sciences", or better still: "the bourgeois ideology of the sciences") are both at the same time said to be rationalized and reified. And when it was said (as Marcuse insisted) that science is the concrete project of society, he would be taking up the Marxist theme of the base superstructure dialectic. On the one hand the sciences are read as objective, being grounded in the site of productive forces of society, and on the other hand, they are understood as *ideological projects*. In this setting what happens is that the sciences in the double occurrence of techne and ideology mime not only the dominant class position, but also the ontological structure of the commodity which is fetishizing at its very essential nature. So when the Frankfurt School, following Lukács, claimed that pure quantification and the negation of qualities (along with the negation of humanity) forms the core of the natural scientific method, then they were emphasizing Marx's claim in

Capital. Marx in *Capital* had said that commodity production negates use-values and consequently also negates qualities. In the quest for realizing exchange value it posits pure quantities. What we are left with is nothing but spectres: *Alle seine sinnlichen Beschaffeneiten sind ausgelöscht*[196]—*all* sensuous conditions are extinguished! After peeling off all materiality, there is only one residue left: "ghostly reality" (*gespenstige Gegenständlichkeit*)[197]. And this ghostly reality will dictate not only the political ideology of capitalist societies but also its technical apparatus. The five points of Lukács' critique of the natural sciences that we noted above are understood in the ontology of the ghostly commodity. The ghostly commodity not only possesses the capitalists but also the scientists. They have become the high priests of the capitalist mode of production.

It is thus that one is able to understand the critique of rationalization as reification of the Frankfurt School. The crisis of the modern sciences would not only be based on what Husserl called the inability for science to tell us anything[198], but also on the will to power—"the need to be authoritative", in Nietzsche's words, "the need not to 'know', but to subsume, to schematize, for the purpose of intelligibility and calculation".[199] Because humanity and nature are split up in the act of commodity production, the will to calculate and control becomes now the leitmotiv of the modern sciences. It also becomes the ideology of societal modernization. The inherent logic of the modern sciences grounded on commodity production and the accumulation of capital is the logic of violence. It is not only the *techne* of the modern science and the telos of Western Reason. It is the *theoria* itself. To question this very basis of Western rationality is now the essential part of radical philosophizing. If the sciences have erased the very telos of humanity, then the point is to put this humanity in the very centre of philosophy.

When it seemed that Platonism and the philosophies of the transcendent "Idea" had been banished by the modern sciences, then it was a mistake, because the mathematization of nature initiated by the modern sciences created a "purely rational, ideational system....the dream", as Marcuse called it, "of all Platonism".[200] This ironic return of idealism was also an ironic end to Western Reason–the fulfilment of its telos as well as its betrayal[201], because reason and theoria develop only as the positive sciences, while philosophy which "was supposed to give the ends, the objectives, the meanings of science" moves into the background.[202] Reason is now divorced, as Marcuse says, from "that rational *humanitas* envisaged in the original philosophical project, scientific, technological rationality becomes reason *Kath' exochen*".[203]

Now not only is the original project of philosophy betrayed, but so are the projects of modernity and the Enlightenment. Modernity is now rationalized modernity–'rationality' now meaning not Reason per se, but capitalist economic activity, bourgeois private law, and bureaucratic authority.[204] So if reason and theoria are reduced to techne, if reason becomes only instrumental reason and if the original idea of philosophy that raised the ideas of truth, beauty and goodness are lost then what we have is the betrayal of the original project of reason–reason exists only in the "name of rationality" which is in the last resort nothing but political domination.[205]

So reason as technological reason or scienticism is strictly speaking neither scientific nor philosophical. Rather it is ideological, ideological because it is conceived as a *social project*.[206] What we get now is technology and technique as independent realms, independent not only from philosophy, but from the sciences themselves. In fact technological reason pretends itself to be 'science'.

For Marxism, the critique of technological reason as the leitmotiv of Western capitalist rationality is not focused on the critique of science, but the regression of the sciences under this ideological project of late imperialism in permanent crises. If scienticism, appearing as the reified spectre is critiqued, then one ought not to fall back on the mythopoetical attack on the sciences themselves. For when one is attacking the crisis-ridden domain of the modern sciences and so-called "Western Reason" (it is best to use the term *"Bourgeois Reason"*), one cannot turn to a fictitious "Eastern Reason" (or any other variation of romantic anti-capitalism) for a mythical solution. For Marx, every society has a tremendous accumulation of the sciences, and as he records in his lesser read *Ethnological Notebooks*, the non-capitalist societies has had a history of scientific reasoning. Yet this uncanny "Eastern Reason" that almost inevitably may arise from the critique of Western Reason, ought to be seen merely as a return of the spectre and delusion haunting class societies. This type of reasoning is the ideology of what Marx preferred calling the ideology of the Asiatic Mode of Production–the economic world of the periphery of international capital accumulation which have lost out to the West, because the West with its most grotesque discovery of capital accumulation colonized it. Colonization is the most important 'scientific' discovery' of the West. Not only is colonization its ideology, but also its theology. If we claimed that Western Reason, as Bourgeois Reason, has two main epistemic points (modern sciences/mythopoetics) then it also has two main geo-political locations: the centre and the periphery. Now this ideology-theology of the West claims that what lies outside its own realm (the 'rest') has to be occupied. In this pyramid made by Bourgeois Reason, the elites of the West stand on top of the pyramid. And most certainly not any form of Eastern Reason, and most certainly any form of idealizing "Indian philosophy" is going to destabilize it.

In anti-thesis to this West/East, science/philosophy, materialism/idealism divide one must recall the symbolic interactive world of Habermas' communicative action. For it is this symbolic interaction that would be able to bridge these great divides. Or else, one will have to "drum dialectics into the heads of the mushroom-upstarts of the new, holy Prusso-German Empire"[207], whereby not only the hegemony of Bourgeois Reason would collapse, but also the hegemony of brother mullah and sister yogi. And that is why I had earlier said that human passion is the basis of Marxist science where we have the following historical reading:

> According to Hegel, all sciences are woven by the thread of the *aufheben*–the logic which raises reality at a higher level of existence. Hegel thought (and falsely so) that his science, his *Wissenschaft*, the *Wissenschaft der Logik*, would be the culminating moment of all the sciences and remain at the centre stage of world history. Little did he know that history would propel a certain Karl Marx who would be waiting in its wings. And with the discovery of the continent of history, he was literally knocking at the doors of world history. It is then that one understands, that at each stage in world history, it is not utopia which is either waiting in the wings, or knocking at its doors, but revolutions, for revolutions (whether in the history of theory or material practice) are simply irresistible.[208]

ENDNOTES

1. Karl Marx and Frederick Engels, 'Manifesto of the Communist Party', in *Marx. Engels. Selected Works* (Moscow: Progress Publishers, 1975), p. 46.
2. Slavoj Žižek, 'A Plea for Leninist Intolerance', in *Critical Inquiry*, Winter, 2002.
3. Jacques Derrida, *Spectres of Marx. The State of the Debt, the Work of Mourning, and the New International*, trans. Peggy Kamuf (New York and London: Routledge, 1994), p. XIX.

4. Slavoj Žižek, 'A Plea for Leninist Intolerance'.
5. See my 'In Defence of Leninism', in *Economic and Political Weekly*, Vol. VLI, No. 1, January 1, 2011.
6. Karl Marx and Frederick Engels, op. cit., p. 40.
7. Ibid.
8. See my 'Leninism as Radical Desireology', in *Economic and Political Weekly*, Vol. XLVI, No. 39, September 24, 2011, p. 66.
9. Marx and Engels, op. cit.
10. Ibid.
11. Slavoj Žižek, 'A Plea for Leninist Intolerance', in *Critical Inquiry*, Winter, 2002. Despite agreeing in a certain way with Žižek, I must firstly intervene by what Lukács said: "There was no hatred in Lenin. He fought against institutions and this, naturally, meant that he also had to fight against the men who represented those institutions–if necessary to their annihilation. But he always considered it a humanly deplorable necessity even though it could not be avoided or disregarded under certain concrete conditions." See Georg Lukács, *Lenin. A Study on the Unity of His Thought* (Cambridge: Massachusetts: The MIT Press, 1974).
12. V.I. Lenin, *What is to be Done?* (Moscow: Progress Publishers, 1978), p. 26.
13. Engels, Frederick, 'The Condition of England. I. The Eighteenth Century' in *Marx and Engels. Collected Works*, Vol. 3 (Moscow: Progress Publishers, 1975).
14. V.I. Lenin, op. cit.
15. Slavoj Žižek, 'A Plea for Leninist Intolerance'.
16. Frederick Engels, 'To Franz Mehring, London, July 14, 1893', in *Marx. Engels. Selected Works* (Moscow: Progress Publishers, 1975), p. 690.
17. See my 'Leninism as Radical Desireology', in *Economic and Political Weekly*, Vol. XLVI, No. 39, September 24, 2011, pp. 64-5.
18. Frederick Engels, 'To Franz Mehring in Berlin', p. 690.
19. V.I. Lenin, *Materialism and Empiro-criticism* (Moscow: Progress Publishers, 1977), p. 320.

20. William Shakespeare, 'Julius Caesar', In *The Complete Works of William Shakespeare* (London: Henry Pordes, 1983), Act I, Sc. II, p. 890.
21. Karl Marx and Frederick Engels, 'Manifesto of the Communist Party', p. 53.
22. Karl Korsch, 'Leninism and the Comintern', in Douglas Kellner, *Karl Korsch. Revolutionary Theory* (Austin & London: University of Texas Press, 1977), p. 152.
23. Karl Marx, *Das Kapital*, Erster Band (Berlin: Dietz Verlag, 1981), p. 88.
24. Slavoj Žižek, *The Sublime Object of Ideology* (London: Verso, 1989), p. 29.
25. See my 'Leninism as Radical Desireology'.
26. Karl Marx, *Economic and Philosophic Manuscripts of 1844* (Moscow: Progress Publishers, 1982), pp. 135-6.
27. Ibid., p. 136.
28. Ibid., pp. 96, 111, 136.
29. See Slavoj Žižek, 'Seize the Day: Lenin's Legacy'.
30. Karl Marx, *Economic and Philosophic Manuscripts of 1844*, p. 120.
31. Quoted in Georg Lukács, *Lenin. A Study on the Unity of His Thought*, p. 94.
32. The first public reaction to the idea of re-actualizing Lenin", as Žižek has recently put it, "is of course an outburst of sarcastic laughter". See Slavoj Žižek, 'A Plea for Leninist Intolerance', where he says that the bourgeois may tolerate Marx as the "poet of commodities", such that Marxism is reified as a culture theoretist", but never Lenin, the Lenin of the revolutionary party. But the first state reaction (which Žižek does not talk of) is outright fear.
33. Karl Marx, *Capital*, Vol. I, trans. Samuel Moore and Edward Aveling (Moscow: Progress Publishers, 1984), p. 80.
34. Karl Marx, *Capital*, Vol. III, p. 830.
35. Ibid., p. 77, pp. 86-7.

36. Karl Marx, *Capital*, Vol. III, p. 830.
37. William Shakespeare, 'Hamlet', in *The Complete Works of William Shakespeare*, Act I, Sc. V, p. 950.
38. Karl Marx, op. cit.
39. Karl Marx, *Economic and Philosophical Manuscripts of 1844*, p. 110.
40. Sigmund Freud, 'The Uncanny', in *The Penguin Freud Library*, Vol. 14, *Art and Literature* (London: Penguin, 1985), p. 339.
41. Ibid., p. 340.
42. Ibid.
43. Ibid., pp. 341-2.
44. Ibid., pp. 342, 346.
45. Ibid.
46. Ibid., p. 347.
47. Ibid., p. 350.
48. Karl Marx, 'Theses on Feuerbach", in *Marx. Engels. Selected Works* (Moscow: Progress Publishers, 1975), p. 28.
49. Ibid.
50. Karl Marx, *Das Kapital*, Erster Band, pp. 56-61.
51. Considering Marx's critique of reification in general then relate this theme of Hamlet-Freud with Marx's critique of philosophy itself. From this we observe that a split takes place and the latter pole of each binary starts operating on its own. But wait! Have we not seen the similar type of critique of philosophy engaged by Marx? Did not Marx in the *Contribution to the Critique of Hegel's Doctrine of the State* critique Hegel for involving the process of inverted thinking? Did not Marx say that Hegel involves a mystification? And is this mystification nothing but an inversion? Does not one relate the mystification and inversion of philosophical thinking expressed as the estranged mind, with the inversion of bourgeois reality itself? Consider Marx, in Hegel the following pairs are inverted: subject/object, being/consciousness, empirical/transcendent, material/ideal, finite/infinite, existence/essence, determinate/determined, etc., to get the reversed pairs:

object/subject, consciousness/being, transcendent/empirical, etc., etc. Now not only is there an inversion, but also an erasure within each of the pairs to posit the world in the "form of the object". What is left is the *transcendent-idealized-essence*. The world appears as the hypostatized estranged signifier. So when Marx says that for Hegel reality appears as "the Idea", claiming to be an "independent subject", and functioning as the "demiurgos of the real world (*der Demiurg des Wirklichen*)", he is saying that Hegel's importance is found in the epistemological process of the mystification-inversion, which is a mere superstructure for a deeper structural inversion. And this inversion implies a "personification of the thing and the reification (*Verdinglichung*) of the person" (*Theories of Surplus Value*, Part I (Moscow: Progress Publishers, 1975), p. 390. We get this: mystification= inversion=reification=dep-ersonification of the human and the personification of the thing. And for Marx, like Freud, the estranged and reified object would turn out to be the source of the distortion and reification of consciousness. In this way, Marx draws the importance of the reading of philosophy (as the estranged mind) so as to look into the estrangement of reality itself. The philosopher as the 'philosopher's philosopher' is now not the disinterested philosopher seeking the philosopher's stone but the ideologist. The philosopher constructs the logic of the reified mind. The ideologist creates the mass consciousness of bourgeois society. In this way the philosopher, both as the 'philosopher's philosopher' as well as the ideologist becomes the embodiment and spokesperson of this distortion and bourgeoisiefication.

52. Johann Wolfgang Von Goethe, *Faust*, trans. Philip Wayne (London: Penguin, 1949), p. 67. For Marx's usage of the same see *Capital*, Vol. I, p. 556.

53. Karl Marx, 'Contribution to the Critique of Hegel's Philosophy of Right. Introduction' in *Karl Marx. Early Writings*, trans. Rodney Livingstone and Gregor Benton (New York: Vintage Books, 1975), p. 244.

54. Ibid.
55. Ibid.
56. Karl Marx, *Capital*, Vol. I, p. 189.
57. Ibid., p. 76.
58. Ibid., p. 58.
59. Sigmund Freud, op. cit., p. 358.
60. Karl Marx, op. cit., p. 81.
61. Ibid., p. 76.
62. Karl Marx, *Capital*, Vol. III (Moscow: Progress Publishers, 1986), p. 830.
63. Karl Marx, *Economic and Philosophic Manuscripts of 1844*, p. 129.
64. Karl Marx, *Das Kapital*, Erster Band, p. 52.
65. Ibid., p. 51.
66. Karl Marx, *Capital*, Vol. I, p. 98.
67. Karl Marx, *The Poverty of Philosophy* (Moscow: Progress Publishers, 1978), p. 52.
68. Karl Marx, *Capital*, Vol. I, p. 79.
69. Karl Marx, 'Contribution to the Critique of Hegel's Doctrine of the State' in *Karl Marx. Early Writings*, trans. Rodney Livingstone and Gregor Benton (New York: Vintage Books, 1975), p. 169.
70. Karl Marx, *Economic and Philosophic Manuscripts of 1844*, p. 131.
71. Karl Marx and Fredrick Engels, *The German Ideology*, p. 68.
72. Ibid., pp. 64, 65.
73. Ibid., p. 61.
74. Karl Marx, 'Contribution to the Critique of Hegel's Philosophy of Right. Introduction', p. 251.
75. Karl Marx, 'Preface', *Contribution to the Critique of Political Economy* (Moscow: Progress Publishers, 1977), p. 22.
76. Kevin Anderson, *Lenin, Hegel, and Western Marxism. A Critical Study* (Urbana and Chicago; Univesrity of Illinois Press 1995).
77. Karl Marx, 'To Engels, London, January 14, 1858', in *Marx. Engels. Selected Correspondence* (Moscow: Progress Publishers, 1975), p. 93.

78. Karl Marx, *Das Kapital*, Erster Band (Berlin: Dietz Verlag, 1981), p. 27.
79. Louis Althusser, *For Marx*, trans. Ben Brewster (London: Allen Lane, 1969), p. 90.
80. Fredrick Engels, 'Feuerbach and the End of Classical German Philosophy', in *Marx. Engels. Selected Works* (Moscow: Progress Publishers, 1975), pp. 589, 590, 591-3.
81. Karl Marx, 'Contribution to the Critique of Hegel's Philosophy of Right. Introduction', in *Karl Marx. Early Writings*, trans. Rodney Livingstone and Gregor Benton (New York: Vintage Books, 1975).
82. Karl Marx, *Economic and Philosophical Manuscripts of 1844*, (Moscow: Progress Publishers, 1982), p. 127.
83. Karl Marx, 'Difference Between the Democritean and Epicurean Philosophy of Nature', in *Marx. Engels. Collected Works*, Vol. 1 (Moscow: Progress Publishers, 1975).
84. Karl Marx, 'To Arnold Ruge' in *Marx. Engels. Collected Works*, Vol. 3 (Moscow: Progress Publishers, 1975), p. 144.
85. Karl Marx, *Economic and Philosophic Manuscripts of 1844*, p. 129.
86. Ibid., p. 131.
87. Karl Marx, *Das Kapital*, p. 27.
88. Ibid.
89. Ibid.
90. Karl Marx, 'Contribution to the Critique of Hegel's Doctrine of the State', in *Karl Marx. Early Writings*, trans. Rodney Livingstone and Gregor Benton (New York: Vintage Books, 1975), p. 62; 'Kritik der Hegelschen Staatsphilosophie' in *Karl Marx. Die Frühschriften*, (Stuttgart: Alfred KrönerVerlag, 1964), p. 24.
91. Karl Marx, 'Contribution to the Critique of Hegel's Doctrine of the State', in *Karl Marx. Early Writings*, trans. Rodney Livingstone and Gregor Benton (New York: Vintage Books, 1975), p. 62; 'Kritik der Hegelschen Staatsphilosophie' in *Karl Marx. Die Frühschriften*, (Stuttgart: Alfred KrönerVerlag, 1964), p. 24.

92. Karl Marx and Fredrick Engels, *The German Ideology* (Moscow: Progress Publishers, 1976), p. 42; 'Die deutsche Ideologie', *Karl Marx. Die Frühschriften* (Stuttgart: Alfred Kröner Verlag, 1964), p. 349.
93. Louis Althusser, *For Marx*, pp. 90, 91,
94. Karl Marx, 'Zur Kritik der Hegelschen Rechtphilosophie. Einleitung', in *Die Frühschriften*, (Stuttgart: Alfred Kröner Verlag, 1964), p. 215.
95. G.W.F. Hegel, *Science of Logic*, trans. A.V. Miller (London: George Allen & Unwin, 1969), p. 107.
96. Karl Marx, 'On the Jewish Question', in *Karl Marx. Early Writings*, trans. Rodney Livingstone and Gregor Benton, p. 216 .
97. Ibid., p. 193.
98. Karl Marx, 'Contribution to the Critique of Hegel's Philosophy of Right. Introduction', in *Karl Marx. Early Writings*, p. 244.
99. Karl Marx, *Economic and Philosophic Manuscripts of 1844*, p. 91.
100. Karl Marx and Frederick Engels, 'Deutsche Ideologie', in *Die Frühschriften*, p. 367.
101. Karl Marx and Frederick Engels, *The German Ideology*, p. 54.
102. Karl Marx, 'Nationalökonomie und Philosophie', in *Die Frühschriften*, p. 235.
103. From this brief note on the question of the dialectic we have noted that three sites have to be transcended–alienation, private property and the state. Later, as we all very well know, Marx talked of the smashing of the state, a theme that Lenin had kept at the centre of his *State and Revolution*, a theme that the parliamentary left has simply forgotten.
104. Karl Marx, *Economic and Philosophic Manuscripts of 1844*, pp. 90, 91, 94, 109, 132, 143, 'Nationalökonomie und Philosophie', in *Die Frühschriften*, pp. 251, 264, 271, 280-81, 282.
105. Karl Marx and Frederick Engels, *The German Ideology*, p. 42.
106. Ibid.
107. Karl Marx, 'Preface', *A Contribution to the Critique of Political Economy* (Moscow: Progress Publishers, 1977), p. 21; 'Zur Kritik

der Politischen Ökonomie. Vorwort', *Marx. Engels. Ausgewählte Schriften in Zwei Bänden* (Berlin: Dietz Verlag, 1979, p. 336.

108. Karl Marx, 'On Hegel', in *Marx. Engels. Collected Works*, Vol. 1 (Moscow: Progress Publishers, 1975), p. 577.
109. Karl Marx, *Economic and Philosophic Manuscripts of 1844*, pp. 70, 71.
110. Karl Marx and Fredrick Engels, *The German Ideology*, p. 49.
111. Ibid., p. 42.
112. Ibid., p. 43.
113. Karl Marx, 'Contribution to the Critique of Hegel's Philosophy of Right. Introduction', p. 249.
114. Louis Althusser, *Lenin and Philosophy*, p. 30.
115. Ibid., p. 31.
116. Karl Marx, op. cit., p. 250.
117. Karl Marx, 'Thesen über Feuerbach', in *Die Frühschriften*, (Stuttgart: Alfred Kröner Verlag, 1964), p. 339.
118. Ibid.
119. Ibid.
120. Karl Marx, *Capital*, Vol. I, p. 77.
121. Ibid.; *Das Kapital*, Erster Band, p. 86.
122. Ibid., p. 27.
123. Karl Marx and Fredrick Engels, 'Manifesto of the Communist Party' in *Marx and Engels. Selected Works* (Moscow: Progress Publishers, 1975), p. 61.
124. Ibid.
125. Ibid.
126. Ibid.
127. See my *The Seductions of Karl Marx* (Delhi: Aakar Books, 2010), p. 208. Riza Davari-Ardakani, Inqilab-I Islami va Vaz'-I Kununi' Alam [The Islamic Revolution and the Current Conditions of the World] (Tehran: Markaz-e Farhangi-I Alame Tabatabai, 1982). Quoted in Farazin Vahadat, 'Post-Revolutionary Islamic Discourses on Modernity in Iran: Expansion and Contraction

of Human Subjectivity', in *International Journal of Middle East Studies*, Vol. 35, November 2003, No. 4, pp. 605, 610.

128. Louis Althusser, *Lenin and Philosophy*, trans. Ben Brewster (London: Monthly Review Press, 1971), pp. 15, 38, 39, 42, 72, 99.
129. Karl Marx, 'Preface to the First German Edition', *Capital*, Vol. I, p. 19.
130. Karl Marx, *Das Kapital*, Erster Band, p. 12.
131. Karl Marx, *Theories of Surplus Value*, Part. I, p. 40.
132. Karl Marx, *Grundrisse*, trans. Martin Nicolaus (London: Penguin, 1974), p. 100.
133. Karl Marx, *Capital*, Vol. I, p. 19.
134. Fredrick Engels, 'Engels to J. Bloch in Konigsberg', in *Marx. Engels. Selected Works* (Moscow: Progress Publishers, 1975), pp. 682-3.
135. Karl Marx, *Capital*, Vol. I (Moscow: Progress Publishers, 1984), p. 19.
136. Karl Marx, 'To the Editorial Board of the *Otechestvenniye Zapaiski*, London, November, 1877', in *Marx. Engels. Selected Correspondence* (Moscow: Progress Publishers, 1975), p. 293.
137. Ibid.
138. Karl Marx, 'To J.B. Schweitzer, London, January 24, 1865', in *Marx. Engels. Selected Correspondence* (Moscow: Progress Publishers, 1975), p. 145.
139. Ibid.
140. Louis Althusser, op. cit., p. 15.
141. Karl Marx, 'To John Baptist Schweitzer, London, January 24, 1865', in *Marx. Engels. Selected Correspondence* (Moscow: Progress Publishers, 1975), pp. 144-5.
142. Karl Marx and Fredrick Engels, *The German Ideology* (Moscow: Progress Publishers, 1976), pp. 51, 61.
143. Karl Marx, *Economic and Philosophic Manuscripts of 1844*, p. 99.

144 Ibid., p. 98.

145. Ibid., p. 99.
146. Ibid., p. 98.
147. Ibid,. p. 94.

148. Ibid., p. 98.
149. Ibid.
150. Ibid.
151. Ibid.
152. Ibid.
153. Ibid.
154. Ibid., p. 99.
155. Karl Marx, 'A Contribution to the Critique of Hegel's Philosophy of Right', in *Karl Marx. Early Writings*, trans. Rodney Livingstone and Gregor Benton (New York: Vintage Books, 1975), p. 251.
156. Karl Marx, 'Afterword to the Second German Edition', in *Capital*, Vol. I, p. 29.
157. Karl Marx, *Economic and Philosophic Manuscripts* of 1844, p. 133.
158. Ibid., p. 132.
159. Ibid.
160. Ibid., p. 136.
161. Ibid., p. 99.
162. Ibid., p. 137.
163. Murzban Jal, 'The Irresistible Science of Karl Marx', in the *Social Scientist*, Vol. 38, Nos. 5-6, May-June 2010.
164. See Slavoj Žižek, 'Seize the Day: Lenin's Day'.
165. Ashis Nandy, 'History's Forgotten Doubles', in *History and Theory*, Vol. 34, No. 2, Theme Issue 34: World Historians and Their Critics. (May, 1995), p. 46.
166. See Peter Hudis, 'Marx Among the Muslims', in *Capitalism, Nature, Socialism,* Dec 2004.
167. See Samir Amin, *Capitalism in the Age of Globalization. The Management of Contemporary Society* (Delhi: Madhyam Books, 1994), pp. 80-90. See also my *The Seductions of Karl Marx*, pp. 25, 81.
168. See my 'In Defence of Marxism: A Reply to a Neo-Hindu's reading of *The Seductions of Karl Marx*', in *Critique*, Vol. 40, No. 1, February 2012.

169. Edward Said, *The Question of Palestine* (New York: Vintage Books, 1992), p. 3.
170. Ibid.
171. Edward Said, *Orientalism. Western Conceptions of the Orient* (London: Penguin, 1995), p. 21.
172. B.R. Ambedkar, 'Annihilation of Caste', in *The Essential Writings of B.R. Ambedkar*, ed. Valerian Rodrigues (New Delhi: Oxford University Press, 2008), p. 267.
173. Karl Marx, 'The British Rule in India', in *On Colonialism* (Moscow: Progress Publishers, 1976), pp. 40-41.
174. See Aijaz Ahmad, *In Theory. Classes, Nations, Literatures* (Delhi; Oxford University Press, 1994), p. 224.
175. Ibid., p. 225.
176. Ibid.
177. Ibid.
178. Karl Marx, 'Letter to Vera Zasulich', in *Marx. Engels. Selected Works*, Vol. 3 (Moscow: Progress Publishers, 1970), p. 154.
179. Karl Marx, *Capital*, Vol. I, p. 76.
180. Ibid., p. 80.
181. Karl Marx, 'To Engels, London, June 14, 1853', in *Marx. Engels. Selected Correspondence* (Moscow: Progress Publishers, 1975), p. 80.
182. Martin Heidegger, 'To Herbert Marcuse, January 20, 1948', in Herbert Marcuse, *Technology, War and Fascism*, ed. Douglas Kellner (London: Routledge, 1998), p. 265.
183. Karl Marx, *Economic and Philosophic Manuscripts of 1844* (Moscow: Progress Publishers, 1982), p. 98; Karl Marx and Fredrick Engels, *The German Ideology*, p. 34, n.
184. Karl Marx, *Economic and Philosophic Manuscripts of 1844* (Moscow: Progress Publishers, 1982), p. 98.
185. Ibid., p. 99.
186. Ibid., p. 92.
187. Ibid., p. 97.
188. Ibid., pp. 97-8.

189. Ibid., p. 98.
190. Ibid.
191. Ibid., p. 97.
192. Georg Lukács, *History and Class Consciousness* (London: Merlin Press, 1983), p. 3.
193. Ibid.
194. Georg Lukács, *The Theory of the Novel*, trans. Anna Bostock (London: Merlin Press, 1994), p. 64.
195. Georg Lukács, *History and Class Consciousness*, p. 202.
196. Karl Marx, *Das Kapital*, Erster Band (Berlin: Dietz Verlag, 1981), p. 52.
197. Ibid.
198. Edmund Husserl, *Crisis of the European Sciences and Transcendental Phenomenology*, trans. David Carr (Evanston. I.U.: Northwestern University Press, 1970), p. 6.
199. Friedrich Nietzsche, *The Will to Power*, trans., Walter Kaufmann (New York: Vintage Books, 1968), p. 278.
200. Herbert Marcuse, 'On Science and Phenomenology', in *The Essential Frankfurt School Reader* (Continuum: New York, 1982), p. 469.
201. Ibid.
202. Ibid.
203. Ibid.
204. Jürgen Habermas, 'Technology and Science as Ideology', in *Towards a Rational Society*, trans. Jeremy Shapiro (London: Heinemann, 1971), p. 81.
205. Ibid., 82
206. Ibid. See also Herbert Marcuse, 'Industrialization and Capitalism in the Works of Max Weber', in *Negations. Essays in Critical Theory*, trans. Jeremy Shapiro (Boston, 1968).
207. Karl Marx, 'Afterword to the Second German Edition', *Capital*, Vol. I, p. 29.
208. See my 'The Irresistible Science of Karl Marx'.